Trading With

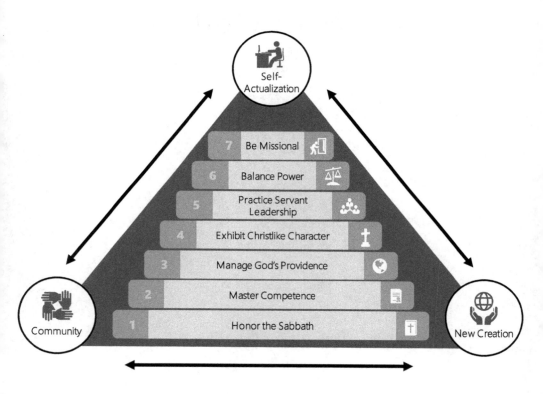

Trading With God

Seven Steps to Integrate Your Faith into Your Work

KEN SNODGRASS

WIPF & STOCK · Eugene, Oregon

TRADING WITH GOD
Seven Steps to Integrate Your Faith into Your Work

Wipf & Stock
An Imprint of Wipf and Stock Publishers
199 W. 8th Ave., Suite 3
Eugene, OR 97401

www.wipfandstock.com

PAPERBACK ISBN: 978-1-5326-8327-5
HARDCOVER ISBN: 978-1-5326-8328-2
EBOOK ISBN: 978-1-5326-8329-9

Manufactured in the U.S.A.   JULY 22, 2019

To Tracy, who walks the bell lap with me

Contents

Illustrations

Preface

LIFE IS A JOURNEY and so is writing a book. What started with a question ended with a book. The first phase was professionally working for thirty-four years after departing my undergraduate university. I had the pleasure of working with so many talented people. My last twenty-four working years were spent with Shell, a company full of creative, competent, and caring professionals around the globe. In many corporations, there are people who don't display the character of servant leadership nor the personal qualities of humility, gratitude, and courage. Fortunately, the vast majority of my former Shell colleagues did exhibit good character and leadership skills.

After retiring, I spent almost two years of full-time study at Austin Presbyterian Theological Seminary. This small seminary, adjacent to the massive University of Texas campus, is an oasis of caring professors, staff, and students. My time there was transformational. Academic Dean Dr. David Jensen is a strong advocate for the Master of Theological Studies (MATS) program. He wrote an excellent book on the theology of work, *Responsive Labor*, and graciously counseled me on researching my capstone paper. He also gave me valuable feedback on an early draft of this book. Dr. William Greenway taught the MATS capstone course and provided me with excellent feedback on my capstone paper and book project. His advice helped organize my research and book format. Dr. Cynthia Rigby and Dr. Paul Capetz opened the theological world to me. Their excellent teaching, feedback, and patience allowed me to read and extract the theological gems of past and present writings. They set high academic standards for their students, which made us more competent in our religious studies. Dr. David Johnson's factual memory was amazing and his teaching fused Christian history with theological concepts. Without understanding the historical context of theology, one cannot truly understand theology. Dr. Timothy Lincoln taught me the theology of money, which infused theology into my business experiences, something that was sorely needed. His course helped shape the *Manage God's Providence* chapter. Dr. Philip Wingeier-Rayo's courses on the missional church put theological concepts into my mission experiences. Compassionate hearts need to be linked to effective strategies. His courses shaped the *Be Missional* chapter. Rabbi Neil Blumofe's Judaism course helped me construct the *Honor the Sabbath* chapter. He is truly a Renaissance man—it is a joy to hear his heavenly singing.

I am indebted to many who gave me feedback along this journey. Dr. Harold Cain, Rev. Bobbi Kaye Jones, and Rev. David Gilliam read and spent several hours of their time with me. They are truly servant leaders. Shell retirees Paul Spicer and Steve Brown were both supportive during my writings and provided feedback, as well as another dear friend, Dr. Tony Stanley. Justin Gould and Jordon Bauchi of the Texas Methodist Foundation (TMF) read an early draft and provided me with excellent feedback. Kelsey Spinnato, a PhD student in Old Testament, helped me with my initial Scripture research and gave advice on publishing. Dr. Ed Berger, President of Southwestern University, provided me with advice on the publication process and was a constant source of support. I am indebted to Veronica Hughes who edited my first draft. Her editorial advice greatly improved my writing skills. Dan Veitkus, author of *Straight Talk Your Way to Success*, kindly recommended Veronica and answered my many questions on publishing.

I am blessed to have supportive family and friends. My prayers each day are filled with heart-filled gratitude for my loving community. The one person who journeyed every day with me was my wife, Tracy. She read each chapter numerous times during the journey and constantly provided constructive criticism. Her advice came strictly out of love, especially given that theology is not her favorite subject! It was her constant support for this project that was truly special. She had to contend with my theological studies, long hours of research, discussions about the book project, the publication process, and the roller coaster of emotions that come during the journey. This book is dedicated to her.

Introduction

I have found that the God who created and sustains the world is also the God of the workplace. If the Christian faith is not relevant in the workplace, it is not relevant at all.[1]

KEN COSTA, FORMER CHAIRMAN OF LAZARD, UK

I therefore, the prisoner in the Lord, beg you to lead a life worthy of the calling to which you have been called. (Eph 4:1)

PAUL THE APOSTLE, ALSO KNOWN AS SAUL OF TARSUS

IN 2011, I WAS working in London, managing Shell's gas and power trading and marketing activities in Northwest Europe. One of my teams was Deal Structuring. This relatively small group (less than ten employees) was composed of analytical professionals, some with PhDs in financial quantitative analysis. These "quants" were brainy techies who spoke in mathematical terms that few people outside of the energy trading business could understand. They were key to our success as a business, and my team greatly relied on their expertise.

Ian (not his actual name), one of the youngest quants, was a British professional in his twenties. He was a quiet, humble employee who did excellent analytical work and exceeded expectations. Ian periodically scheduled meetings with me to review contract valuations or to answer one of my questions. At one meeting in 2011, he came into my office and we sat together with the door closed so I could concentrate on his presentation.

1. Ken Costa, *God at Work*, 1.

At the end of the review, I sat back and asked Ian how he was doing. Did he find his work satisfying, and was he growing professionally in his current job? One of my managerial roles was to mentor high-performers like Ian, and I used our remaining time together to steer his development. Ian replied that, professionally, all was going well. He liked Shell and said that he stayed very busy. Ian was cheerful during our discussion, so I surmised that all was going well. But then his expression changed, and he said, "Can I ask you a personal question?" I replied, "Sure, no problem."

Ian looked squarely at me and said, "I know that you are a Christian. Can I work for Shell and still be a Christian?"

Although I knew from trading floor discussions that Ian was an observant Christian, we had never talked about our shared faith. His question stunned me. It had never occurred to me that working for Shell was inconsistent with my Christian faith. However, I had never given his question any thought during my more than thirty years of professional employment.

After a moment of silence, I responded, "Why do you ask this question?"

Ian replied, "I am not sure that God values the work I do at Shell. It seems to me that other occupations are more valuable to God."

"If you mean church work," I said, "do you feel called to work in the church, perhaps as an ordained clergy?"

Ian stated that he felt no call for church work: "Using my financial skills to evaluate trading contracts just seems to me not as worthy as other professions." Although Ian enjoyed his work, he did not believe that his application of quantitative and financial skills in a trading environment was something God desired of him.

I asked, "And what skills or occupations does God desire of you?"

Ian shook his head. "I don't know. I was hoping that after your many years of working for Shell in energy trading, you would have already worked through my question and found a landing place."

Frankly, I had never considered this question and lamely answered, "Christians are needed in the workplace now more than ever. Christianity is in decline in Europe. Shell's role is to efficiently and safely deliver energy to our customers. Energy has made the world a better place to live and is a necessary part of our modern existence. Trading's role is to maximize Shell's contractual value so that the profits can be reinvested to solve future energy needs. This is a worthy occupation, no different from other purposeful occupations. Your professional skills are needed, along with your faith. I have never thought that what I do in my Shell job goes against God's wishes, and I believe that my faith is exhibited at work just as it is at church or home."

Ian nodded and thanked me, then left my office. I shut my door and sat looking out my window overlooking the Thames River, watching the masses of people walking around the Embankment Gardens. After over fifty years of being a Christian, I realized that I didn't understand the theology of work and faith. Even worse, I didn't even think to ask the hard questions. I was unprepared for Ian's question, and I had failed him. I had punted a quick answer without deeply understanding how my day-to-day job linked to my faith. During my decades of going to church and reading Scripture and numerous Christian books, I had not addressed this central and vitally important question: *Is the Christian faith relevant in the workplace, and if so, how?*

Holy Trinity Brompton Church, London

Shortly after my conversation with Ian, my wife and I were attending a Holy Trinity Brompton (HTB) Sunday morning service. The speaker that week was Ken Costa, then Chairman of Lazard, an investment banking company. Investment bankers provide financial advice and services to companies, governments, and nonprofits. Here was a highly successful investment banker preaching in the Church of England—something I had never envisioned!

After church, I googled Ken and discovered that he had written a book, *God at Work*, and I bought a copy at the HTB bookstore the following week. This was the first book I had read that discussed faith and work. HTB also offered a course on faith and work, one of many diverse HTB educational courses designed to link faith with relevant topics such as marriage and parenting. HTB membership has grown immensely over the past twenty years because this church makes Christianity relevant to modern lives and is externally focused.

Life After Shell

During the next couple of years, I was wrestling with what to do with my life post-Shell. Ian's question kept haunting me, and I believed that the church lacked an effective education program that articulated the theology of faith and the workplace. I had plenty of experience in the workplace.

What I lacked was the theological education. I needed to combine these two seemingly separate worlds, secular and sacred, to effectively understand this highly relevant topic.

After deciding to retire in Austin, Texas, I applied to Austin Presbyterian Theological Seminary (APTS), located only ten minutes from our home. I was accepted into the two-year Master of Theological Studies (MATS) program and begin classes in the fall of 2014. Three months after retiring from a thirty-four-year energy career, I was a full-time student carrying a small backpack full of textbooks. My wife joked that I looked like our grandson who was starting pre-school. On the first day of classes, I thought, "What have I got myself into?"

About 60 percent of the MATS curriculum was composed of courses like Old/New Testament, theology, Christian history, etc. I was allowed significant freedom to select elective courses that interested me and increased my understanding of faith and work. While there were no specific courses on the theology of work, my final capstone paper was a comparison of the work theologies of John Calvin and Karl Barth. It was a delightful discovery that the APTS Dean of Faculty, Dr. David Jensen, had authored a book called *Responsive Labor*, and was a theologian who deeply understood the theology of work. His guidance was most helpful for my capstone paper, as was the encouragement and feedback received from my capstone professor, Dr. William Greenway.

This book highlights my journey over more than four years. Given 2,000 years of Christian history and a growing publication of books on faith in the workplace, I soon realized that there was no lack of research on my chosen topic. I felt that a practical book that fuses workplace practices with scholarly theology would be helpful, as most available publications focus on one or the other. My intent is to provide a framework that can be put into daily use in the workplace.

The Disconnect: Secular and Sacred

So why was a lifelong Christian like me lacking in even the most basic knowledge on faith in the workplace? I discovered that I was not alone. Surveys conducted by Mark Greene, Director of the London Institute for Contemporary Christianity (LICC), provide some alarming statistics:

- 50 percent of Christians have never heard a single sermon on work.

- Over 70 percent have never been taught a theology of work.

- Fewer than 25 percent have ever been asked by their minister about their witness at work.[2]

The only time I ever heard a sermon on faith and work was a recent sermon on Labor Day in my Austin church. Until I attended HTB, I had never seen a church course advertised on the theology of work. I had never observed a minister at my office, never been asked by a minister to visit me at my office, or discussed workplace issues with a pastor. Except for my capstone class at seminary, there were never any lectures, discussions, or reading assignments on the theology of work.

Why is "faith and work" such an invisible topic within the church? My research uncovered many reasons, and here are a few:

> Part of the reason theologies of work get so little attention is that the gatekeepers of theology are mostly clericalized professionals, few of whom have spent their lives—or else forgotten—working in factories, raising crops, or in other ways affording themselves a laboring layperson's point of view. Indeed, the conventional wisdom of church professionals perfunctorily screens out or only nods at the seemingly secular world and its occupations . . . Nevertheless, the laity constitute that part of the church that serves the world, and that role demands recognition.[3]

> "Professional Christian work" was somehow more spiritual, a higher calling, the place where you could really serve God and others, and thus become more Christlike. Ordinary, daily, mundane work was at best a mission field, and at worst a distraction in the spiritual life.[4]

> Antipathy between clergy and businessmen is a venerable American tradition. It is, in fact, a common phenomenon within the history of Christianity more broadly, which some would trace to Christ's own sayings on money and his violent overturning of the moneychangers' tables in the temple in Jerusalem. An attempt to understand the historical conflict between business and religion must take into account longstanding tensions between business people and clergy.[5]

2. Scurlock and Goss, *I Love My Work*, 9–10.

3. Larive, *After Sunday*, 63.

4. Cosden, *Theology of Work*, xv.

5. See Kevin E. Schmiesing, in Capaldi, *Business and Religion*, 90.

Many Christian clergy do not understand the struggles that their laypeople who work in the marketplace face in integrating their faith and their work.[6]

History has shown that, if left to the church professionals alone, there will never be much of a ministry in daily life for most of the Christians in America. Putting aside a small minority of ordained ministers who are threatened by the principle of a universal priesthood, most church professionals support a ministry of the laity in principle but do not know *how* to equip people for ministry in daily life. The reason is perfectly understandable.[7]

Amazingly little theological reflection has taken place in the past about an activity [work] that takes up so much of our time.[8]

Faith and Work—A Long History

The topic of faith and work has been a major theme since the earliest of biblical writings. Christian theologians have been writing about the theology of work since the early church period after the New Testament was compiled, and it remains a topic of study. The theology of work evolved over time as workplaces and cultures changed; this is no different from other theological fields of study. Secular and sacred relationships have also evolved over time, as God's revelations have continued to reform humanity.

This book is not an indictment against the church or those professionals who faithfully serve within the church, but I do hope it will enlighten the organized church. I strongly believe in Christian community worship, prayer, discipleship, and service. I have witnessed the faithful service of the clergy who use their God-given talents to take our world closer to the kingdom. In seminary, I witnessed faculty, staff, and students struggle with difficult theological subjects, wrestle with complex texts, and study for long hours while working and/or parenting. I found my fellow seminary students were entering ministry because of their love for Jesus Christ and their desire to uplift their community with words of hope, acceptance, and love. I commend and honor them for their commitment to serve God and their communities. My hope is that this book will assist them in their ministry.

6. Hicks, *Religion and the Workplace*, 131.

7. Diehl, *Monday Connection*, 181.

8. Volf, *Work in the Spirit*, 69.

Who Should Read This Book?

This book is meant to help working Christians on their journey of faith within the workplace, regardless of where you are along the journey. Faith journeys can range from the early questions ("Who is Jesus?") to much deeper theological questions. Parts I and II are more theological and theoretical. Part III is more practical.

This book is also meant for clergy and church workers (teachers, missionaries, administrators) who need educational resources on the subject of faith and work, whether for themselves, their church congregations, and/ or their larger communities. The bibliography and cited references can also assist with any further research.

Organization of the Book

This book is divided into three major parts. Part I gives an overview of the history of faith and work, beginning with Scripture, both Old and New Testaments, proceeding from the early church period to our modern times. All Scripture quotes are from the New Revised Standard Version (NRSV) Bible, unless otherwise stated. A helpful glossary of terms is located in Appendix B. After the Scripture chapter, I cover each historical Christian period by selecting one or more theologians who wrote about the theology of work during that time. I specifically quote from these theologians so you can hear their voices. I summarize each theologian's important contributions to the theology of work at the end of each chapter. My intention is to help the reader understand the issues that each theologian encountered and how the theology of work changed over time. This will offer a historical overview that is foundational to the current theology of work. Theologians typically build their theology with the beneficial hindsight of past theologians; I will follow this trend. If part I proves too theological for your tastes, then begin with part II.

Part II develops a simple, three-part theological model of work and faith. The model is explained in detail and was developed from my research. I was particularly drawn to several modern and postmodern reformed theologians: Karl Barth, Jürgen Moltmann, David Jensen, Miroslav Volf, and Darrell Cosden. However, my writings were influenced by many other outstanding theologians and authors who trailblazed work theology. My simple theological model of work should be used in the workplace just as a technical person applies mathematical models to solve problems. It is an application tool, but you must still prayerfully make all workplace decisions. You now have a compass to help you find the right path.

Part III presents seven steps built from the theological model described in part II. This section is the most practical, filled with personal stories that illustrate the model in practice, with advice from many sources. Following these seven steps will build a strong foundation for being obedient Christians in the workplace. My book will not guarantee you a promotion or more money, although I predict that if you apply my ideas, you will be more centered in your faith during your working life. May it bring joy and peace to those who yearn to walk with Christ in the workplace.

PART I

The History of Christian Faith and Work

The Early Church (Creation–313 CE)

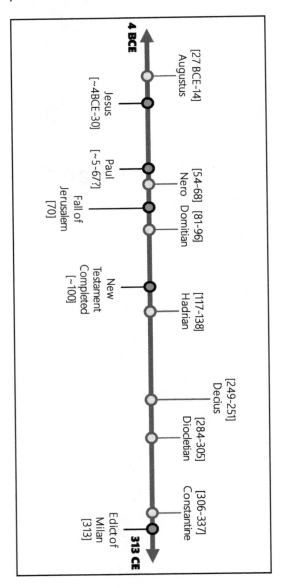

Figure 1—The Early Church Timeline

Scripture

THE STORY OF CHRISTIANITY begins with God's creation as told in Genesis. Scripture continues with a description of God's relationship with his chosen people. God, in freedom, reveals and establishes covenants. The Bible is a theological book written by humans who were inspired by the Holy Spirit. It contains theology, history, prophesies, poetry, wisdom, and truths. It is the primary authority upon which the Christian faith seeks God's eternal revelations.

The biblical stories, starting with Abraham, began before the pre-state tribal period (1250–1000 BCE).[1] Scholars debate about the exact dating of the early Hebrew biblical patriarchs since there is no known archeological evidence. Perhaps with more scientific and archeological research, the early Hebrew patriarchal period will be better determined. Until then, Scripture is our only guide.

Before the fall of the First Jerusalem Temple in 586 BCE, the Hebrew Bible (Old Testament) as we know it was not written down, with the exception of some fragmented parts.[2] The Hebrews were exiled in Babylon after 586 BCE, and most biblical scholars agree that the Hebrew texts were compiled after the Hebrews returned to Jerusalem in the postexile period, starting in 538 BCE.[3] The last Old Testament books, Ezra through Nehemiah, date to the mid-second century (160–150s BCE).[4]

There was more than a 200-year gap in Scripture between the Old Testament writings and the gospel writings. Mark, the first written Gospel, was completed about thirty years after Jesus' resurrection during the reign

---

1. Carr, *Introduction to the Old Testament*, 25.
2. Carr, *Introduction to the Old Testament*, 198–99.
3. Carr, *Introduction to the Old Testament*, 25.
4. Carr, *Introduction to the Old Testament*, 259.

of Nero (54–68 CE), and Revelation, the last New Testament book, was completed during the reign of Domitian (81–96 CE).[5] The twenty-seven books, as listed in our present New Testament, were compiled and authorized by the church during the fourth century CE in reaction to different heretical Christian beliefs. Today, there are numerous translations of the original Hebrew, Greek, and Aramaic Scriptures. Scholars continue to debate the exact wording of the texts since the original texts were handwritten and eventually lost. Although we are blessed today with excellent scholarly translations and biblical research, there are still many unanswered questions about the contextual meanings. I doubt that all biblical questions will ever be answered. God's revealed word is a part of our journey of faith.

Scripture is the primary reference that Christians should examine relating to their work and faith. In this chapter, I will show that *Scripture is filled with the lives of working people and their work*. Faith and work is an important theme of the Bible. For some, this may come as a surprise. The subject of faith and work is rarely discussed in many churches.

During biblical times, work was important, as it put food on the table, provided security, educated future generations, and increased competencies. In some ways, the ancient Hebrew and Christian communities worked like our contemporary communities: farming, mining, manufacturing, fishing, trading, teaching, performing, governing, leading, serving, etc. What has changed is the requisite skills and scale of our work. For example, computerization and automation have replaced manual labor and the use of rudimentary tools. Human work occupies most of our waking hours, just as it did during biblical times.

Work-Related Statistics

I will statistically show just how much of Scripture is devoted to work, although my analysis is not exhaustive of Scripture references on work. Using BibleWorks,[6] a computerized biblical research tool, I developed a Scripture database of work-related words from Scripture to highlight how often work is referenced in the Bible. I transferred the verses to a spreadsheet and analyzed them to validate that the word was indeed work-related and, if so, who or what was working. I counted how many times these work words

5. González, *Story of Christianity*, 1:8.
6. BibleWorks, Version 10, Norfolk, VA.

were used in the Old and New Testament in relationship to human work. My major assumptions:

1. Only human work is counted. Work related to nonhuman beings (God, animals, angels, etc.) is excluded.

2. The work relationship must be to an occupation. For example, *gathering a crop* is work-related, while *gathering people together* is not.

3. Each word is counted. If the word is used more than once in a verse, all are counted.

4. The New Revised Standard Version (NRSV) is the chosen translation. Other English Bible translations will have different word counts, although the differences will be minor.

5. The word counts are separated into two groupings: occupations (typically nouns) and actions (typically verbs). For example, *worker* was placed in the occupation listing and *working* was placed in the action listing. These two listings are further separated into the Old and New Testament word counts. The nineteen books of the Apocrypha are not included.

6. Similar words are grouped together into a single word count. For example, *worker, workers, workman,* and *workmen* are grouped together for a total word count.

7. While I tried to capture all the words related to work, the list is not comprehensive. Some may disagree on the exact word interpretations or word counts. I do not believe my conclusions will change based on others' statistical analysis and different word counts.

8. Words related to the military, like *fighting,* are excluded. I wanted to be conservative even though in contemporary times military service is considered an occupation.

9. I did not include hereditary positions such as *king* as occupations. Although they greatly influenced history and human lives, they correspond to a very small number of people.

10. I included spiritual occupations such as *priests* and *rabbis.*

There are 745,598 words in the NRSV Bible: 569,174 (76 percent) in the Old Testament, and 176,424 (24 percent) in the New Testament. Only about 2 percent (16,538) of the 745,598 words in Scripture are unique; words such as *the, and,* and *I* are very common.

Biblical Occupations

There are 1,908 (79 percent) occupation-related words in the Old Testament, and 505 (21 percent) in the New Testament, roughly proportional to the word count in the Old and New Testaments. Agricultural occupations have a high word count, as demonstrated in Figure 2. Given that the majority of biblical people worked in agriculture, this makes sense.

Agriculture Occupations	Old Testament	New Testament	Total
Worker	32	8	40
Shepherd	29	11	40
Laborer	16	8	24
Reaper	11	1	12
Sower	2	7	9
Farmer	7	1	8
Herder	6	-	6
Vinedresser	5	-	5
Tiller	4	-	4
Hewer	3	-	3
Treader	3	-	3
Grape-gatherer	2	-	2
Harvester	1	-	1
Planter	1	-	1
Plower	1	-	1
Total	123	36	159

Figure 2—Agricultural Occupations

Appendix A charts all the other occupations included within Scripture:

- Service (majority of people employed)
- Government (administered community policies and governmental laws)
- Religious
- Artisan and Manufacturing (buildings and households)
- Nautical (fishing and travel)
- Leadership and Managerial
- Business and Professional (schools and legal)
- Musical and Visual Arts

Work-Related Biblical Words

Scripture is full of words that describe how people worked: 1,820 (79 percent) words are found in the Old Testament, and 496 (21 percent) are found in the New Testament. Seven general work-related words and their associated derivatives dominate the word count and are shown in Figure 3. Building projects are emphasized more in the Old Testament than in the New Testament.

General Work	Old Testament	New Testament	Total
Build	309	26	335
Work	233	81	314
Teach	58	80	138
Labor	62	17	79
Toil	42	9	51
Burden	27	13	40
Task	12	5	17
Total	743	231	974

Figure 3—General Work

The remaining charts of work-related words are shown in Appendix A. These include:

- Agricultural Work
- Business-Related Work
- Artisan and Manufacturing Work
- Management and Government Work

Given the amount and diversity of work-related words, it is reasonable to state: *Scripture is filled with words and stories about people at work.*

Scripture Verses that Relate to Work Attributes

I downloaded and reviewed over 6,000 Scripture verses during my word search. After completing the statistics, I highlighted verses that relate to the seven work attributes developed in part III. Here are just a few of the many verses that support these attributes:

Competence

- "He has filled them with skill to do every kind of work done by an artisan or by a designer or by an embroiderer in blue, purple, and crimson yarns, and in fine linen, or by a weaver—by any sort of artisan or skilled designer" (Exod 35:35).
- "Therefore command that cedars from the Lebanon be cut for me. My servants will join your servants, and I will give you whatever wages you set for your servants; for you know that there is no one among us who knows how to cut timber like the Sidonians" (1 Kgs 5:6).
- "According to the grace of God given to me, like a skilled master builder I laid a foundation, and someone else is building on it. Each builder must choose with care how to build on it" (1 Cor 3:10).

Providence

- "They would give the money that was weighed out into the hands of the workers who had the oversight of the house of the LORD; then they paid it out to the carpenters and the builders who worked on the house of the LORD" (2 Kgs 12:11).

- "There is nothing better for mortals than to eat and drink, and find enjoyment in their toil. This also, I saw, is from the hand of God" (Eccl 2:24).

- "The one who plants and the one who waters have a common purpose, and each will receive wages according to the labor of each" (1 Cor 3:8).

Character

- "You shall not withhold the wages of poor and needy laborers, whether other Israelites or aliens who reside in your land in one of your towns" (Deut 24:14).

- "Moreover, it is required of stewards that they be found trustworthy" (1 Cor 4:2).

- "Now such persons we command and exhort in the Lord Jesus Christ to do their work quietly and to earn their own living" (2 Thess 3:12).

Leadership

- "Let them sit as judges for the people at all times; let them bring every important case to you, but decide every minor case themselves. So it will be easier for you, and they will bear the burden with you" (Exod 18:22).

- "She rises while it is still night and provides food for her household and tasks for her servant-girls" (Prov 31:15).

- "Pay to all what is due them—taxes to whom taxes are due, revenue to whom revenue is due, respect to whom respect is due, honor to whom honor is due" (Rom 13:7).

In summary:

- From biblical times to the present, God's word is eternal. Scripture is the primary authority for the Christian faith.

- Scripture is filled with stories about the lives of working people.
- Scripture reveals that work is an important part of the journey of faith.
- Work attributes (part III) are supported by Scripture.

The Imperial Church (313–450)

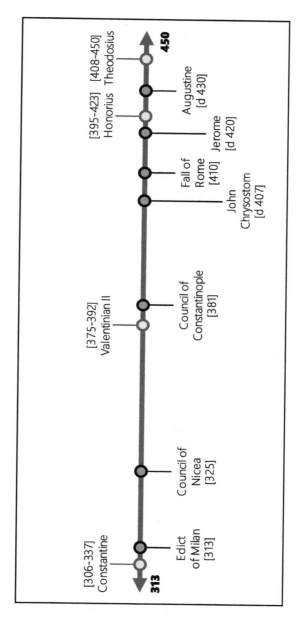

Figure 4—The Imperial Church Timeline

Theology

Theology does not just belong within the pious sanctum of the churches. Its place is the public market places of the different cultures as well. It is in the mental and spiritual conflicts of contemporary life that Christian anthropology must prove its truth, a truth that leads to real humanity.[1]

—*JÜRGEN MOLTMANN,*
PROFESSOR EMERITUS OF SYSTEMATIC THEOLOGY

THEOLOGY IS A DISCUSSION about God to understand God's revelation to humans. It is *faith seeking understanding*. It comes from the Greek word *theologia,* meaning God (*theos*) speech (*logos*). For many, it is a dry and dense subject, but I invite you to relax and lighten up for theology demands an open mind!

I went to seminary primarily seeking answers to my many spiritual and scriptural questions and to study the great theologians. After two years of intense studies, many of my questions were answered, but I left with many more. This is the nature of theology, or *faith seeking understanding*. We can never know everything about God because God is so much greater than humans and reveals only what God decides to reveal about God's nature. However, we are called as faithful Christians to spend our lives seeking understanding. One of my seminary professors stated that all Christians become theologians through the study of God.

Most Christians view theology as something for pastors and scholars to study, a subject for lecture halls and debates. I disagree. There are jewels to be found within those massive theological volumes. With the help

1. Moltmann, *On Human Being*, ix.

of a theological dictionary and a Bible, any Christian can read the great theologians. This will help shape and refine your beliefs. For example, even *disagreeing* with a theologian will enable you to better articulate what you believe.

My two years of studies were necessary for me to research theological writings on faith and work. Although I had read Scripture and numerous religious books, I was not classically educated in theological studies and decided to enroll in seminary. Austin Presbyterian Theological Seminary was fortunately only a few miles from our Austin home and has an excellent academic reputation.

During my first year of seminary, I took two foundational theology courses. Systematic theology deals with theological thinking and practice in an orderly, coherent way. Each week, we studied a different theological concept, such as Christology (the study of Jesus Christ) and eschatology (the study of the end of the world). Reading a wide range of theological publications on each concept helped me understand a wider breadth of viewpoints.

During the second semester, I studied six theologians in depth. Every two weeks, I intensively focused on one theologian—his or her faith journey, beliefs, and major writings. For each, I wrote a short paper on that theologian's views. It goes without saying that to condense a loquacious theologian's writings down to a few typed pages is a major feat. However, the exercise gives you an excellent understanding of that person's views.

For our final exam, I was required to state my own theological beliefs, citing two theologians who supported and two who opposed my ideas. So, for the first time—after a year of theological study and reading thousands of pages of others' thoughts—I was asked to state *my own* faith beliefs. After a year of study, it was very satisfying to find that the final exam wasn't as difficult as I'd anticipated because my educational journey helped me clarify my opinions. I had found my comfort zone along the wide theological spectrum.

Theologians have written extensively about faith and work. In the first part of this book, we'll explore the theology of work developed after the Gospels were published. It was during the imperial church era—from Constantine (306 CE) to the fall of Rome (410 CE)—when the first post-apostolic theology of work writings were published.

I've used particular quotes from major theologians—some from the past, some living—so you can hear their voices. This book is not a comprehensive review, but it conveys the major theological concepts about faith and work. Walk through Christian history with me and see how the relationship between the church and the working world has changed over time. My hope is that the journey will enlighten you.

The first Christian theologian—and in my opinion, the greatest—was the apostle Paul (5–64CE), born Saul of Tarsus. Thirteen of the twenty-seven New Testament books are attributed to Paul. In addition, we learn about Paul's missionary travels in the Acts of the Apostles. All we know about Paul's life and theology is contained in the New Testament. Paul's writings about human work will be extensively analyzed in this book through the writings of other theologians. Therefore, I have not devoted a chapter specifically to Paul's writings.

John Chrysostom (349–407)—
The First Developed Theology of Work

What then is the greeting? *Greet Priscilla and Aquila,* he says, *my fellow-laborers in the Lord.*[1]

AFTER THE GOSPELS WERE published, Christianity grew rapidly, as did periods of persecution. Christians were torn between accepting martyrdom or accepting secular norms. As Justo González wrote: "Many found an answer in the monastic life: to flee from human society, to leave everything behind, to dominate the body and its passions, which give way to temptation."[2] For solitude, the early monastics mainly chose the desert, especially in Egypt. The word *monk* is derived from the Greek word *monachos*, which means "solitary." The early monastic movement was not a church-authorized movement, but an individualized movement of hermits. Their goal was to live a solitary existence devoted to prayer, contemplation, and penance. Two famous hermits were Paul and Anthony. Paul's life was documented by Jerome, who translated the Greek Bible into Latin. Athanasius, the archbishop of Alexandria, told the story of Anthony's life.[3]

But how could a Christian practice love while living a solitary life? Other monks decided that communal living was the answer. They still lived a relatively solitary life away from the world, but with a community of fellow contemplative Christians. They shared property and lived in poverty, and they set up discipline and rules to enforce the contemplative life. In

---

1. Kroeger, "John Chrysostom's First Homily," 16.
2. González, *Story of Christianity*, 1:158.
3. González, *Story of Christianity*, 1:161–65.

most cases, they chose a leader. They worked communally, but in a spiritual manner, usually singing or chanting prayers. Through pilgrimages and publications, word spread of the holy monastic life, and the hierarchical church began to first notice and then admire the monastic ideals.[4] Over time, the church took control of the monastic life as it spread through the Christian world.

Theologians have debated whether a Christian should live the active life or the contemplative life ever since the monastic movement began during the early church period. This monastic movement was important for the theology of work because it was the first time that Christians withdrew from the secular community and confined themselves to a contemplative Christian life. Devout Christians viewed work as a non-Christian part of life, as opposed to a total concentration on the spiritual life. The superior choice was either to not work and be supported by others, or work just enough to survive. The lifestyles of monks were so spartan that many ruined their health.

John Chrysostom's life and beliefs exemplified this conflict. He was born into a Christian family in Antioch (near the modern city of Antakya, Turkey) and received an excellent education. When he announced that he intended to leave home and become a monk, his mother objected, so he lived at home with an ascetic lifestyle until her death. He then joined a small group of monks in the Syrian wilderness. After six years, when the ascetic lifestyle had taken a harsh toll on his health, he returned to Antioch to recover. He was ordained as a deacon, and his fame spread due to his outstanding preaching skills. When the position of archbishop of Constantinople became vacant in 397, the emperor offered him the job. Chrysostom fought abuses, both within the church and against state rulers, and this eventually led to his exile and death.

Chrysostom "gives the first developed Christian theology of work." According to Eric Osborn, a professor of the New Testament and early church history, Chrysostom "defends the importance and dignity of work; man belongs to the material world in which he has been placed."[5] His theology is based on the creation story found in the Old Testament, and he places rest after work.

In Chrysostom's *First Homily on the Greeting to Priscilla and Aquila*, he outlined his theology of work. The sermon was based on Romans 16:3,

4. González, *Story of Christianity*, 1:165–72.

5. Osborn, *Ethical Patterns*, 121–22.

which says, "Greet Prisca [Priscilla] and Aquila, who work with me in Christ Jesus." To fully understand this sermon, some background information is needed on Priscilla and Aquila. They were friends of the apostle Paul in Corinth (Acts 18:1–3). Aquila was a Jew who had been expelled from Rome with other Jews by the AD 19 edict of Claudius (Acts 18:2). From Rome, Priscilla and Aquila went to Corinth, where they met Paul and worked with him making tents. They accompanied Paul when he left Corinth, and they remained in Ephesus after he returned to Syria (Acts 18:18–19). When Paul wrote the First Letter to Corinth, they were still at Ephesus, where Christians gathered in their home (1 Cor 16:19). They later lived in Rome (Rom 16:3) before returning to Ephesus (2 Tim 4:19).[6]

Theology of Work

Chrysostom divided his theology of work into four major elements. First, there was dignity in work. Priscilla and Aquila worked with Paul as tentmakers. They were not ashamed of working or supporting themselves even though Roman culture held that work was for lower classes and slaves, not for nobility and the wealthy. Chrysostom viewed work as noble through the acts of these devout Christians. "Clearly he [Paul] knew, that virtue in lifestyle, rather than splendor of wealth or abundance of riches, was wont to produce nobility."[7]

Second, Chrysostom stated that the spirituality exhibited in the work of Priscilla and Aquila exceeded that of those living the monastic contemplative life. "Nothing could equal this in a reckoning of excellence."[8]

Third, Chrysostom cited the working life of Abraham that enabled him to show hospitality to those in need. Christians are called to share and open their homes to strangers in need.[9]

The fourth component—and the bulk of his sermon—was devoted to the sin of idleness. Chrysostom supported his argument with the Genesis creation story and the active life of Paul. In Genesis 1:11, God created the vegetation "but he commanded that produce should be brought forth from the earth through our labors, so that you might learn that he introduced work because of the advantage and benefit to us." While God's commanding

6. Comfort and Elwell, *Complete Book of Who's Who*, 499–500.
7. Kroeger, "John Chrysostom's First Homily," 17.
8. Kroeger, "John Chrysostom's First Homily," 17.
9. Kroeger, "John Chrysostom's First Homily," 18.

humans to work by the "sweat of your face" (Gen 3:19) may seem harsh and punishing, it was "produced by sin." Chrysostom then ties Genesis to the labor Paul undertook to avoid being a burden to the Christian community (1 Thess 2:9 and Acts 20:34): "A man who gave commands to demons, who was the teacher of the civilized world, who was entrusted with all those who dwell upon the earth, and all the churches lying under the sun, and ministered with great solicitude to peoples, and nations and cities—this man worked night and day."[10] If the apostle Paul worked to support himself and his community, then Christians should follow his example and not be idle.

This was an outstanding defense of the active life, especially from a bishop who lived in a monastery! To develop his theology of work, Chrysostom must have worked during his monastic period and practiced what he preached. And (as described in the pages ahead) more than a thousand years later, another monk followed Chrysostom's path out of the monastery into the active life—and reformed the world.

Favored the Priesthood over Secular Life

But which profession was better for serving God: the priesthood, including the monastic life, or a secular occupation? Chrysostom clearly favored the priesthood:

> Let the distinction between the pastor and his charge be as great as that between rational man and irrational creatures, not to say even greater, inasmuch as the risk is concerned with things of far greater importance.[11]

Chrysostom, in his second letter to Theodore, who had fallen away from the priesthood, discussed the distractions of domestic life, including the stress and labor required to deal with a wife, children, and domestic workers. He cried out: "Is this then life, Theodore, when one's soul is distracted in so many directions, when a man has to serve so many, to live for so many, and never for himself?"[12] The stresses of family life have not been removed since Chrysostom wrote this letter.

Theologian Dr. Ian Hart wrote: "In the writings of Chrysostom . . . there is an even wider gap between monk and layman; only the monastery

10. Kroeger, "John Chrysostom's First Homily," 19–20.

11. Chrysostom, *Select Library,* 9:40.

12. Chrysostom, *Select Library,* 9:115.

and the priesthood represent serious obedience to and service of God."[13] Already the imperial church was making divisions between sacred and secular work. This division grew wider as the church became more powerful.

I view Chrysostom as conflicted in his desire to be obedient to God through asceticism and his study of Scripture. He preached on the spirituality of work found in the early Christians, yet he elevated the clergy above other professions. This struggle continues today with some Christians. Was my seminary education better in God's eyes than my business or engineering education? Is becoming a minister better than serving society as a public school teacher? Should those who live only a spiritual life be supported by others working in the community? In the next chapter, St. Augustine had to deal with this question while he was Bishop of Hippo.

In summary, Chrysostom:

- Developed the first Christian theology of work using Old and New Testament Scripture:

    1. There is dignity in work.

    2. There is spirituality in work.

    3. Work enables Christians to show hospitality to those in need.

    4. It is sinful to be idle.

- Favored the priesthood over the secular life, thus setting hierarchies between sacred and secular professions.

13. Hart, "Martin Luther," 47.

Augustine of Hippo (354–430)— Work and Pray

Paul the Apostle enjoins and beseeches you in the Lord, that with silence, that is, quietly and obediently ordered, ye do work and eat your own bread.[1]

AUGUSTINE OF HIPPO WAS a western contemporary of Chrysostom. He lived in the northern Africa town of Hippo (modern city of Annaba) in the present country of Algeria. Augustine taught grammar and, after converting to Christianity and becoming a priest, he was appointed the Bishop of Hippo. He led a monastic life even after rising to a high leadership position within the church. His most famous writings are two books: *City of God* and *Confessions*. His theology still influences both Catholics and Protestants.

A church controversy arose in 401 CE as to whether monks should do work. Dr. Osborn highlights the issue: "Many monks did no work and claimed that it was inconsistent with their profession. Augustine attacks their position and defends the dignity of work."[2] In response to a request from the Bishop of Carthage to settle the question of whether monks should work, Augustine wrote *Of the Work of Monks*. The monks were using the words of Christ to support their idleness:[3]

> Therefore I tell you, do not worry about your life, what you will eat or what you will drink, or about your body, what you will wear. Is not life more than food, and the body more than clothing? Look at the birds of the air; they neither sow nor reap nor gather into

1. Augustine, *Select Library*, 3:522.
2. Osborn, *Ethical Patterns*, 155.
3. Augustine, *Select Library*, 3:503.

barns, and yet your heavenly Father feeds them. Are you not of more value than they? And can any of you by worrying add a single hour to your span of life? And why do you worry about clothing? Consider the lilies of the field, how they grow; they neither toil nor spin, yet I tell you, even Solomon in all his glory was not clothed like one of these. But if God so clothes the grass of the field, which is alive today and tomorrow is thrown into the oven, will he not much more clothe you—you of little faith? Therefore do not worry, saying, "What will we eat?" or "What will we drink?" or "What will we wear?" For it is the Gentiles who strive for all these things; and indeed your heavenly Father knows that you need all these things. But strive first for the kingdom of God and his righteousness, and all these things will be given to you as well.

So do not worry about tomorrow, for tomorrow will bring worries of its own. Today's trouble is enough for today (Matt 6:25–34).

Defense of Work Based on the Life of the Apostles

Augustine developed his defense of work by diving into what the apostles said about work in the New Testament. Very early in the Acts of the Apostles, the Christians were indeed a community. "All who believed were together and had all things in common; they would sell their possessions and goods and distribute the proceeds to all, as any had need" (Acts 2:44–45). Augustine wanted the monks to live like the apostles. He says, "Speaking, moreover, of the saints who had sold all that they had and distributed the same, and were dwelling at Jerusalem in an holy communion of life, not saying that any thing was their own, to whom all things were in common."[4] The apostles worked, lived in community, and shared.

Following Chrysostom, Augustine supported his main argument that the monks should work by examining the apostle Paul's life and words. His primary source was his first letter to the Corinthians:

> This is my defense to those who would examine me. Do we not have the right to our food and drink? Do we not have the right to be accompanied by a believing wife, as do the other apostles and the brothers of the Lord and Cephas? Or is it only Barnabas and I who have no right to refrain from working for a living? Who at any time pays the expenses for doing military service? Who plants

4. Augustine, *Select Library*, 3:512.

21

a vineyard and does not eat any of its fruit? Or who tends a flock and does not get any of its milk?

Do I say this on human authority? Does not the law also say the same? For it is written in the law of Moses, "You shall not muzzle an ox while it is treading out the grain." Is it for oxen that God is concerned? Or does he not speak entirely for our sake? It was indeed written for our sake, for whoever plows should plow in hope and whoever threshes should thresh in hope of a share in the crop. If we have sown spiritual good among you, is it too much if we reap your material benefits? If others share this rightful claim on you, do not we still more?

Nevertheless, we have not made use of this right, but we endure anything rather than put an obstacle in the way of the gospel of Christ. Do you not know that those who are employed in the temple service get their food from the temple, and those who serve at the altar share in what is sacrificed on the altar? In the same way, the Lord commanded that those who proclaim the gospel should get their living by the gospel.

But I have made no use of any of these rights, nor am I writing this so that they may be applied in my case. Indeed, I would rather die than that—no one will deprive me of my ground for boasting! If I proclaim the gospel, this gives me no ground for boasting, for an obligation is laid on me, and woe to me if I do not proclaim the gospel! For if I do this of my own will, I have a reward; but if not of my own will, I am entrusted with a commission. What then is my reward? Just this: that in my proclamation I may make the gospel free of charge, so as not to make full use of my rights in the gospel. (1 Cor 9:3–18)

Augustine wrote that Paul was a "chaste evangelist" since he worked with his own hands to live and did not "sell the Gospel."[5] Paul echoed the message of his first letter to the Corinthians in his second letter:

Did I commit a sin by humbling myself so that you might be exalted, because I proclaimed God's good news to you free of charge? I robbed other churches by accepting support from them in order to serve you. And when I was with you and was in need, I did not burden anyone, for my needs were supplied by the friends who came from Macedonia. So I refrained and will continue to refrain from burdening you in any way. (2 Cor 11:7–9)

5. Augustine, *Select Library*, 3:512.

Augustine referenced Paul's letters to the Thessalonians to support his case that monks should work:

> You remember our labor and toil, brothers and sisters; we worked night and day, so that we might not burden any of you while we proclaimed to you the gospel of God. (1 Thess 2:9)

> Now we command you, beloved, in the name of our Lord Jesus Christ, to keep away from believers who are living in idleness and not according to the tradition that they received from us. For you yourselves know how you ought to imitate us; we were not idle when we were with you, and we did not eat anyone's bread without paying for it; but with toil and labor we worked night and day, so that we might not burden any of you. This was not because we do not have that right, but in order to give you an example to imitate. For even when we were with you, we gave you this command: Anyone unwilling to work should not eat. For we hear that some of you are living in idleness, mere busybodies, not doing any work. Now such persons we command and exhort in the Lord Jesus Christ to do their work quietly and to earn their own living. Brothers and sisters, do not be weary in doing what is right. (2 Thess 3:6–13)

Augustine praised Paul for spreading the gospels and working with his hands.[6] Augustine then stated his verdict on those who used Matthew 6 as the basis for not working:

> But when a man says, "This is true righteousness, that by doing no bodily work we imitate the birds of the air, because he who shall do any such work, goes against the Gospel:" whoso being infirm in mind hears and believes this, that person, not for that he so bestows all his time, but for that he so erreth, must be mourned over.[7]

Following Matthew 6 literally meant dying from want of food. For those that put away nothing for tomorrow through their labors will not maintain their life.[8]

6. Augustine, *Select Library*, 3:511.

7. Augustine, *Select Library*, 3:515.

8. Augustine, *Select Library*, 3:518.

Monks Were Running Away from Work

So why did monks not want to work? Augustine speculated in *Monks* that the monks are "running away empty from a poor and laborious life" and "want to be fed and clothed." The monks cannot state that they are not able to work, so they use "ill scholarship."[9]

Balancing the Spiritual and Working Life

Augustine stressed the importance of balancing the contemplative and active lives. He believed both could be combined and he highlighted examples from the lives of secular workers. Workers can sing divine songs and pray while working with their hands, "like as rowers with a boat-song, so with godly melody cheer up their very toil."[10]

Urging a Return to the Early Christian Church

Augustine urged the church and the monasteries to return to the ways of the early Christian church when there wasn't a hierarchical church structure and the Christian leaders worked while spreading the gospel message and forming Christian communities. Understandably, the Protestant Reformation leaders felt connected to Augustine's theology since it was based on Scripture and the early church life.

I can relate to Augustine since he first worked as a teacher and lived the ordinary working life. He struggled with his faith and eventually made the decision to be obedient to Christ. I accepted Christianity from my childhood, but it took many working years to understand what it means to be a follower of Christ when working in the secular world. For all his brilliant theology, Augustine was a practical man who understood human nature. I find common ground with the practical side of Augustine.

Augustine lived just long enough to learn that the Visigoths took over Rome in 410 CE. Vandals sacked Rome in 455 CE, and Romulus Augustulus, the last western Roman Emperor, was deposed by Odoacer in 476 CE. This marked the end of the imperial church and the beginning of the Medieval Church. Dr. Justo L. González, a Cuban-American Methodist historian, states:

9. Augustine, *Select Library*, 3:516.
10. Augustine, *Select Library*, 3:514.

It would be a long time before Western Europe could once again experience the political unity and relative peace that it had known under Roman rule. It would also take centuries to rebuild much that had been destroyed, not only in terms of roads, buildings, and aqueducts, but also in terms of literature, art, and knowledge of the physical world.[11]

It would take a reformation to resurrect Augustine's theology of work.

In summary, Augustine:

- Used the life of the apostles to counter monks who did not want to work:

  1. The early apostles worked, and monks should emulate them.

  2. The apostle Paul worked and supported himself while spreading the gospels rather than burden the community.

  3. If the monks literally follow Christ's words, they will die from the lack of food.

- Speculated that the monks were running away from work by choosing the spiritual life.

- Stressed balancing the spiritual and working lives by combining them.

- Urged the church to return to the early church period and remove the hierarchical structure that separated the sacred and secular professions.

11. González, *Story of Christianity*, 1:260.

The Medieval Church (450–1517)

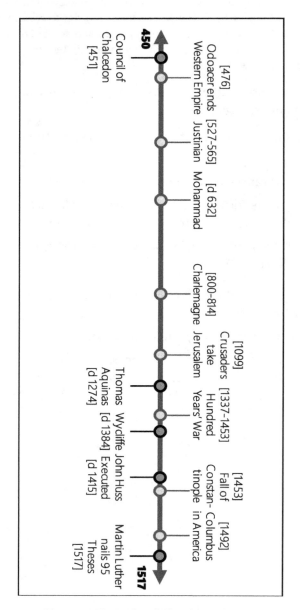

Figure 5—The Medieval Church Timeline

Thomas Aquinas (1225–1274)—
Active Versus Contemplative Life

On the other hand, the active life is more directly concerned with the love of our neighbor, because it is *busy about much serving* (Luke x. 40).[1]

BY THE MEDIEVAL TIMES, the church had taken over the monasteries. German Protestant theologian Dr. Ernst Troeltsch writes:

> However hard monasticism might struggle for a certain measure of independence, and however undefined had been its relationship with the Early Church, in the Mediaeval Church it was organized first of all under the bishops, and then, when the Religious Orders came into existence, under the Papacy; every other kind of asceticism either was, or then became, heretical.[2]

As the gospels spread through Europe and the ancient world, Christianity began to organize hierarchically; first, into congregations, and then parishes, dioceses, provinces, and nations. Civic and ecclesiastical, although serving different purposes, were united. The church and state were one. The offices of priests and bishops became powerful as they had state support. The division between clergy and laity grew wider. A dividing wall was set up between the people and the ministrations of the clergy. The church became involved in politics and had corrupting influences. Their charitable mission was replaced by the benevolent state.[3] Monasteries spread throughout Christendom and were one of the few remaining centers of learning.

1. Aquinas, *Summa Theologica*, 2:1944.
2. Troeltsch, *Social Teaching of the Christian*, 241.
3. Moltmann, *Coming of God*, 165–66.

The Catholic Church considers Thomas Aquinas to be their greatest theologian. He lived in Italy during the medieval period and was a Dominican friar and priest. His theological masterpiece was *Summa Theologica,* which is still taught in seminaries. The book was written using scholastic theology, the formal theology of the medieval period, which is based heavily on debate-style logic, philosophy, and precise language. (Personally, I found scholasticism tedious and confusing, even as an engineer who was trained to think logically. It's like sitting in a lecture room with two dry old men debating an esoteric point in great detail.)

Theology of Work

Aquinas believed in natural theology, the knowledge of God available to human reason through God's revelation in nature. In volume III of *Summa Theologica,* he used natural theology to support differences in vocations in his matrimony and nature section:

> Human nature has a general inclination to various offices and acts, as already stated. But since it is variously in various subjects, as individualized in this or that one, it inclines one subject more to one of those offices, and another subject more to another, according to the difference of temperament of various individuals. And it is owing to this difference, as well as to Divine providence which governs all, that one person chooses one office such as husbandry, and another person another. And so it is too that some choose the married life and some the contemplative. Wherefore no danger threatens.[4]

Aquinas debated four articles in his Question 182 (vol. II): "Of the Active Life in Comparison with the Contemplative Life." The fourth article discussed the following question: "Whether the Active Life Precedes the Contemplative?" He answered with natural law:

> With regard to its nature; and in this way the contemplative life precedes the active, inasmuch as it applies itself to things which precede and are better than others, wherefore it moves and directs the active life. For the higher reason which is assigned to contemplation is compared to the lower reason which is assigned to action.[5]

4. Aquinas, *Summa Theologica,* 3:2713.
5. Aquinas, *Summa Theologica,* 2:1942–46.

In Aquinas's system, the church follows natural law in its institutions, organizations, and values. The natural stage in human life prepares the way for the higher contemplative life. Laypeople have their place within the church, but it is a subordinate place, below the sacred.[6]

Spiritual Life is Superior to Secular Life

In the medieval church, theology was firmly rooted in a two-tiered system: the higher, contemplative occupations (monks, priests, bishops, etc.) and the lower, active occupations (lay businesses). Laypersons *did* have a role— to preserve and procreate human life, something celibate priests cannot (or should not) do: "This is the reason for the enormous gifts and endowments to monasteries; men wanted to make certain of their own part in the oblation offered by monasticism."[7]

This two-tier structure, active versus contemplative, caused tension to develop between laypersons and the clergy. When the European universities were established with the study of Scripture in the original languages, questions were raised about the active-contemplative hierarchy. This became a major issue debated during the Reformation, which was ignited by Martin Luther.

In summary, Thomas Aquinas:

- Based his theology on natural law, using human reason.

- Supported the two-tier active-contemplative hierarchy with the spiritual life superior to lay occupations.

- Supported the active life to preserve and procreate life.

6. Hart, "Martin Luther," 47.

7. Troeltsch, *Social Teaching of the Christian*, 242.

The Reformation (1517–1648)

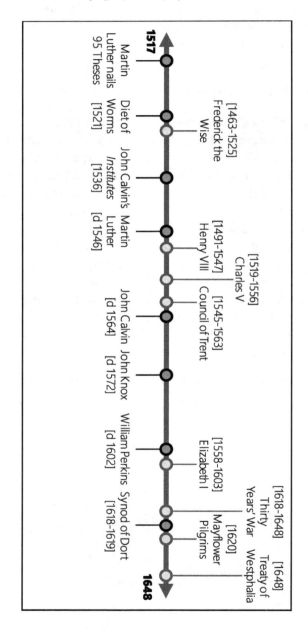

Figure 6—The Reformation Timeline

Martin Luther (1483–1546)—Here I Stand

All works are of equal value.[1]

MOST PEOPLE ASSOCIATE MARTIN Luther with his October 31, 1517 posting of the 95 Theses on the Wittenberg University church door, or his standing firm on his theology of justification by faith in front of the Diet of Worms on April 18, 1521. While these two dates in history are certainly the tipping points of the Protestant Reformation, Luther's theology of work is the tipping point in the history of work theology.

Luther started his educational journey by studying law, but in a life-changing moment, he entered an Augustinian cloister and became a monk. He graduated with a PhD in theology in 1512 and taught at the University of Wittenberg. Through his study of Scripture, he realized that his contemplative life was not superior to the active life. Essentially, he rejected his own vocation as a monk as well as the contemplative life. This theological shift challenged the medieval church and ushered in the Reformation, which dramatically and permanently changed Western Christianity.

This chapter outlines Luther's theology of work, vocation, Sabbath, relationship to government, and business ethics.

Theology of Work

Luther based his theology of work on both the Old and New Testaments. Humans are called to work and not be idle; thus, he rejected the monastic

1. Luther, *Luther's Works*, 44:32. Subsequent references to Luther's Works will be designated as *LW*.

or contemplative vocations. He expressed these views during his lectures on Genesis and commentaries on 1 Corinthians while teaching at Wittenberg University:

> God assigns to Adam a twofold duty, namely, to work or cultivate this garden and, furthermore, to watch and guard it. Some traces of this assignment remain in the wretched remnants we possess. Today, too, these two things must be done together; that is, the land is not only tilled, but what has been tilled is also guarded . . . Man was created not for leisure but for work, even in the state of innocence. Therefore the idle sort of life, such as that of monks and nuns, deserves to be condemned.[2]

Luther uses Lot's management of his household as an example of godly people doing secular work according to his calling. These activities "are more desirable than all the works of all the monks and nuns" and were needed to sustain life. God commanded humans to work and would not have recorded these activities in Scripture if they were unimportant.[3] Then Luther directs his anger at religious orders: "They are like a lazy rogue who does not exert himself bodily but lets others work for him, filling his belly through the sweat and blood of others." Although they sing and do spiritual duties, this does not please God. "Such things, because they are done without His command, cannot please Him."[4]

Luther reinforced his Old Testament theology with the apostle Paul's statements on work. Following Augustine, Luther quotes 2 Thessalonians 3:10 and states, "It is not fitting that one man should live in idleness on another's labor, or be rich and live comfortably at the cost of another's hardship, as it is according to the present perverted custom." He does exempt the clergy who preach and minister to the community, quoting 1 Corinthians 9:14, "on account of their spiritual labor."[5]

Luther did not reject making time for contemplation, but placed it secondary to the active life that served the community: "For Christ at the last day will not ask how much you have prayed, fasted, pilgrimaged, done this or that for yourself, but how much good you have done to others, even to the very least [Matt. 25:40, 45]."[6]

2. *LW* 1:102–3.
3. *LW* 2:349–50.
4. *LW* 28:20–21.
5. *LW* 44:190–91.
6. *LW* 44:71.

Priesthood of All Believers

Luther used 1 Peter 2:9 ("But you are a chosen race, a royal priesthood, a holy nation") as his scriptural support that all Christian work that supported the community and aided the kingdom of the world was of equal value to God. From this came the foundational Protestant doctrine of the "Priesthood of All Believers." The separation of the clergy and laypersons resulted in the "detestable tyranny of the clergy over the laity." The consecrated clergy use their power "to exact, to threaten, to urge, to oppress, as much as they please." If all baptized are equal before God, then the power dynamics are balanced and through "common consent, they would then know that they have no right to rule over us except insofar as we freely concede it." All people are priests and some Christians are chosen as ministers.[7]

Luther asks: How are some Christians chosen as priests if all laypersons are priests? He answers that "we cannot all publicly minister and teach." Humans have different skills. Ministers "of the Word serve others and teach them the faith of Christ and the freedom of believers."[8]

Two Kingdoms

To fully understand Luther's work theology, we must understand that Luther divided his theology into two kingdoms: God's (spiritual) and the world's (temporal or earthly). He writes:

> There are two kingdoms, one the kingdom of God, the other the kingdom of the world . . . God's kingdom is a kingdom of grace and mercy, not of wrath and punishment. In it there is only forgiveness, consideration for one another, love, service, the doing of good, peace, joy, etc. But the kingdom of the world is a kingdom of wrath and severity. In it there is only punishment, repression, judgment, and condemnation to restrain the wicked and protect the good. For this reason it has the sword, and Scripture calls a prince or lord "God's wrath," or "God's rod" (Isa 14 [:5–6]) . . . Now he who would confuse these two kingdoms—as our false fanatics do—would put wrath into God's kingdom and mercy into the world's kingdom; and that is the same as putting the devil in heaven and God in hell.[9]

7. *LW* 36:112–13.
8. *LW* 31:356.
9. *LW* 46:69–70.

In the kingdom of God, only faith matters. Luther spent his early life trying to please God by being a perfect monk, as he believed that God expected him to be perfect. When Luther realized that he could not be perfect, he hated God, as he saw God as an abusive master who judged and punished when perfection was not achieved. Once Luther studied Romans, he realized that, through faith, God justified humans and extended grace. Therefore, works had no place in the kingdom of God. Swedish theologian Dr. Gustaf Wingren wrote: "Conscience rests in faith in God, and does nothing that contributes to salvation; but the hands serve in the vocation which is God's downward-reaching work, for the well-being of men. From the viewpoint of faith, vocation has no relevance."[10] God does not need human work to love and forgive humans.

In the kingdom of the world, our work is directed toward our neighbor (community) and has nothing to do with salvation. In his comments on the Sermon on the Mount, Luther asks the secular community to put Scripture to work in your occupation as "it teaches and preaches how you should treat your neighbor." Use your working tools "in your relations with your neighbor just as you would want your neighbor to use his property in his relations with you."[11] In *The Freedom of a Christian*, Luther writes:

> A man does not live for himself alone in this mortal body to work for it alone, but he lives also for all men on earth; rather, he lives only for others and not for himself. To this end he brings his body into subjection that he may the more sincerely and freely serve others.[12]

Vocation

After we understand the two kingdoms that Luther's theology of work operates within, the next step is to understand his definition of vocation. Dr. Wingren, who wrote *Luther on Vocation*, explains:

> *Vocatio* can mean different things. It can refer to the very proclamation of the gospel, through which human beings are called to be the children of God. It can also be used as meaning the work which each one does as farmer, craftsman, etc. This use of the term

10. Wingren, *Luther on Vocation*, 11.

11. *LW* 21:237.

12. *LW* 31:364.

occurs in I Cor 7:20, where it is said that each shall remain in the same vocation (*klēsis*) in which he was called."[13]

Our modern-day definition of vocation usually denotes an occupation. For example, when I meet someone and am asked about my profession, I typically answer, "I worked as an engineer or energy trader." But Luther's definition of vocation is broader and includes the home life. It includes biological orders (father, mother, son, daughter, etc.). There is no separation between the home and office lives. Luther believes that we are all bound in relationship with each other. Christians occupy a multitude of offices at the same time.[14]

Luther believes that each person is called by God to their assigned vocation according to their abilities. Each person's duty is to toil "happily in accordance with your assigned task and to leave other things to other people." Individuals are to be happy, "but in such a way that you abide in your assigned place."[15]

God's calling to a vocation is for the well-being of the community and not related to salvation, which resides in God's kingdom. This would mix the kingdom of God and the kingdom of the world. Dr. Wingren wrote:

> If I find myself an occupant of some of these life stations which serve the well-being of others, I must not entertain the slightest doubt of God's pleasure, but believe the gospel. The significant thing is not whether I enter such a station as one who is sinful and worthless. The issue is whether the "station" itself is sinful or not ... Therefore a person must avoid stations which are sinful.[16]

It is God who is supporting our called vocation. Without God's gifts, our work would amount to nothing. He uses Genesis 3:19 ("By the sweat of your face you shall eat bread") as support that God commands us to work to survive, but we are not to depend solely on our diligence to survive. "More than our hands is necessary. God must bless and prosper it, and then mightily defend it against all devils."[17]

Luther lived at the end of the socially divided medieval period. Although Luther believed that all temporal works were equal in God's view,

13. Wingren, *Luther on Vocation*, 1.

14. Wingren, *Luther on Vocation*, 4–5.

15. *LW* 15:98.

16. Wingren, *Luther on Vocation*, 4.

17. *LW* 14:122–23.

he also believed that people are called to different vocations depending on their social level:

> Thus it has come about that they say to the pope and his crowd, "*Tu ora*, thou shalt pray"; to the emperor and his servants, "*Tu protege*, thou shalt protect"; to the common man, "*Tu labora*, thou shalt work," not however as though everyone were not to pray, protect, and work. For the man who is diligent in his work prays, protects, and works in all that he does. But everyone should have his own special work assigned him.[18]

Although Luther supported stratified social levels, a common trait in sixteenth-century Europe, he states that all should serve their neighbor and be considered equals. He further states that all workers should be happy regardless of the occupational position assigned to them. "Thus he would also be glad to be a servant if this were God's will. The same thing applies to other stations in life."[19]

Because Luther believed God calls people to assigned vocations, that also meant a person should not change their position. Workers should be satisfied serving their neighbor through their *lifetime* calling. Thus, changing one's calling goes directly against God and shows a distrust of God. Any attempts to rise above one's modest or proper position "is nothing but greed and unbelief."[20]

Binding individuals to called vocations will be brought into question during the industrial and modern ages. During Luther's life, changing one's vocation was extremely difficult since the majority of workers were illiterate and usually inherited their trade from their families. This bound them to their born social status, which was also the norm during medieval times.

Sabbath

Luther supported the Sabbath as a day of rest and a holy day. It should be a day of celebration and community worship. He separated the days of work from the day of rest just as he divided the kingdom of the world and the kingdom of God. Rest is needed for two reasons. First, bodily rest from labor allows the community to "gather in church, see mass, hear God's word,

18. *LW* 44:157.
19. *LW* 30:124.
20. *LW* 44:192.

and offer common, single-minded prayer together." Spiritual rest allows God to "work in us and that in all our powers do we do nothing of our own."[21] In his *Treatise on Good Works*, Luther writes about the Sabbath as the day that God rules:

> This is what it means to observe the day of rest and keep it holy. It is then that a man ceases to rule his own life, then that he desires nothing for himself, then that nothing disturbs him: God himself leads him. It is then that there is nothing but godly happiness, joy, and peace, and all other works and virtues as well. God considers these works so great that he commands us not only to keep the day of rest, but also to hallow it or regard it as holy.[22]

Support for Government

Luther used Romans as scriptural support for Christians to obey their earthly governments. The Reformation movement was dependent on the governmental leaders supporting their cause, and Luther used the apostle Paul's writings (Rom 13:1–7) to back his political need for governmental protection. Paul advocated Christians being subject to governmental authorities and Luther instructed his readers to "obey their will freely and out of love."[23]

However, Luther drew the line when governmental authorities commanded Christians to perform tasks that violated God's commands. Then, "obedience ends and the obligation ceases. In such a case, a man has to say what St. Peter said to the rulers of the Jews, 'We must obey God rather than men' [Acts 5:29]." If a governmental ruler commands an unrighteous war, then Christians are not to follow "because God had commanded us not to kill our neighbor or do him a wrong." The same goes for the other of God's commandments.[24] There was no separation of church and state in Europe during Luther's lifetime, so the church could influence governmental authorities to obey Christian ethics.

21. *LW* 44:71–72.
22. *LW* 44:77–78.
23. *LW* 31:369.
24. *LW* 44:100.

Business Ethics

How Christian workers ethically conduct their work is fundamental to the Christian faith. Theologians are not normally trained economists. Luther was no exception, but from his extensive writings on business ethics, it is obvious that he knew much about the business practices of his day. Luther's father was an industrialist who prospered in his regional mining business. Luther witnessed his father's business dealings with employees and merchants. Certainly the crude language of the workers found its way into Luther's writings!

Before entering the monastery, Luther trained to be a lawyer, and thus understood business contracts. It is my opinion that Luther understood business practices better than most theologians. Reading Luther's writings about business ethics from a modern capitalistic perspective, we can quickly identify his faulty economic premises. However, if we apply biblical concepts to Luther's business ethics writings and view them within his sixteenth-century economy, then he was ahead of his time. From my perspective, Luther's heart was in the right place even though some of his economic beliefs are not valid for a modern capitalistic economy.

The majority of Luther's writings on business ethics were contained in his 1524 publication *Trade and Usury*. His primary focus was marketplace abuses. Luther wrote: "It is our purpose here to speak about the abuses and sins of trade."[25] He wrote it to influence government authorities to take action after "the failure of the diets of Nürnberg in 1522 and 1524 to deal effectively with the monopolistic practices of the trading companies."[26] Here are the major business subjects that Luther commented on:

- Trade
- Pricing Goods
- Surety and Exchanging Goods
- Borrowing
- Trading Merchants
- Anti-Competition

    1. Cornering the Markets

25. *LW* 45:247.
26. *LW* 45:240.

2. Under Selling

3. Colluding

4. Forward Selling

- Bankruptcy and Courts
- Usury
- Passive Investing
- Dishonest Business Practices
- Treatment of Employees

Community was always a focus of Luther's theology, and his writings on business ethics were for the protection of the community. One example was his stand against collusion between merchants. It was anti-competitive for buyers or sellers to meet as a group and decide on buying or selling tactics, such as pricing, quantity, and quality. Luther was against this practice which placed him well ahead of his time.[27]

Excessive Living

The Reformation brought social changes and the belief that Christians were to live moderately. Living in community and helping one's neighbors meant that personal finances needed to be prudently managed. Luther wanted Christians to dress and eat without excess. He wanted the German people to produce all their own food, clothing, and wares, and to halt the costly import of expensive goods. Luther was not against trading between people, but he wanted it limited to strictly local resources.[28] However, modern studies show that international trading has lowered the cost of goods and supported peace between trading nations. The world has prospered through expanded trade. I believe that Luther's heart was in the right place and he wanted his German community to live modestly. Modest living versus materialism is still a subject of debate in modern times.

Martin Luther was a giant figure in world history, not just Christian history. With his mighty stand against the institutional church, he ushered in sorely needed reforms. His scholarship and brilliant writings enabled

27. *LW* 45:266.
28. *LW* 44:212–14.

the masses to be illuminated by Scripture and to think theologically for themselves. Of all the premodern-era theologians that I have read, Luther's writings are the most understandable and practical. This is why his works were best sellers during his lifetime. He understood the German people and the average laborer.

Like all humans, Luther was not perfect. He was fully human with human faults. Nazis used his late writings on the Jews during the twentieth century to justify their inhuman actions. Luther's writings against the church and selected individuals were crude and outrageous, even by today's standards. He was passionate to the point of stubbornness, which precluded other early Protestant reformers from finding common ground and uniting with him in addressing the broken Catholic Church.

Luther did shift the medieval theology of work back to its apostolic roots and equalized the active life of laypersons with the contemplative life of the clerics. Obedience to God meant that workers were to serve their neighbor when operating in the kingdom of the world, but they did not have to work to obtain salvation. It took a French theologian, John Calvin, to organize Protestant theology into systematic completeness to seal the Reformation that Luther started.

In summary, Luther:

- Used both the Old and New Testament to support his theology that humans are called to work and not be idle.

- Opposed the church's two-tier hierarchy and argued that all work that supported the community and aided God's kingdom was of equal value to God.

- Developed a theology on vocations: God called each person to an assigned *lifetime* vocation.

- Supported the Sabbath as a day of rest and a holy day of community worship.

- Required Christians to support their government except when it requested them to violate God's commands.

- Developed a detailed set of business ethics to protect the community from unfair or dishonest business practices.

- Believed that Christians should dress and eat without excess.

John Calvin (1509–1564)—
The Protestant Systematic Theologian

Even the artisan with the humblest trade is good at it only because the Spirit of God works in him. For though these gifts are diverse, they all come from the one Spirit; it pleased God to distribute them to each one.[1]

A DEGREE IN ENGINEERING helped me relate well to John Calvin, as he is extremely thorough and exacting. As one of my theology professors said during class one day, "Calvin doesn't miss much!" She was right!

Calvin was born in 1509 in Doyon, France, into a family that served the bishop. He initially learned the law and later studied theology in Paris. We don't know much about his inner struggles with the Catholic Church, but he left France early in his adult life (1535) and went into exile in Switzerland because of his theological beliefs. Although he desired a scholarly life, he eventually became a community leader and pastor. His publication of *Institutes of the Christian Religion* in 1536 virtually rocked the Christian world. The publication laid out, for the first time, a Protestant systematic theology that organized theology into coherent doctrines of the Christian faith. According to Dr. Justo González:

> The entire work shows a profound knowledge, not only of Scripture, but also of ancient Christian literature—particularly the works of Augustine—and of the theological controversies of the 16th century. There is no doubt that this was the high point of Protestant systematic theology at the time of the Reformation.[2]

1. Hart, "John Calvin," 127.
2. González, *Story of Christianity*, 2:80.

41

Theology of Work

John Calvin developed his systematic theology in Geneva during the early days of the Reformation, and his arguments were constructed as a response to the Catholic Church's dogma. He wrote expansively on the theology of work founded on the Genesis story of the fall of Adam:

> Cursed is the ground because of you; in toil you shall eat of it all the days of your life; thorns and thistles it shall bring forth for you; and you shall eat the plants of the field. By the sweat of your face you shall eat bread until you return to the ground, for out of it you were taken. (Gen 3:17–19)

This curse on work has a pedagogic value, helping man to see his true condition and leading him to repentance.[3]

Calvin then tempered God's curse with God's graciousness using Psalm 127:2: "It is in vain that you rise up early and go late to rest, eating the bread of anxious toil; for he gives sleep to his beloved."

Calvin developed his Doctrine of Providence using Psalm 8:5–8, where God gave humans dominion over the earth, crowning humanity with "glory and honor." Ronald S. Wallace, a former professor of biblical theology at Columbia Theological Seminary, illuminates Calvin's theology:

> The whole of the world is arranged and established for the purpose of conducing to the comfort and happiness of men . . . We must really feel that whatever we enjoy from the hand of God is indeed our rightful heritage, not because we are worthy of it, but because God has elected us to such enjoyment. What we eat and drink must be to us a token of the fatherly love and care of God.[4]

Humans should receive God's gift of earthly providence with joy and thanksgiving, not because they deserve such a gift due to their sinfulness, but because God loves humanity.

Calvin used Scripture to assert that everything God created is good, as stated in 1 Timothy 4:4–5: "For everything created by God is good, and nothing is to be rejected, provided it is received with thanksgiving; for it is sanctified by God's word and by prayer."

Therefore, God has directed our work to be a divinely blessed vocation:

3. Hart, "John Calvin," 122.
4. Wallace, *Calvin's Doctrine of the Christian*, 130–35.

To labour is to fulfill the gracious order of nature, which is planned according to the image of God. Moreover, in our earthly toil not only does the call of God reach us so that toil becomes a divine vocation directed by Him, but also the hand of God is stretched out to us assuring us that our labor will bear fruit.[5]

Protestant Work Ethic

Calvin's emphasis on work as a divine vocation that bears fruit led to the formation of the Protestant work ethic. He wrote: "Labor is often excessively hard and unrewarding, nevertheless we must remember that we were created by God for the purpose of being strenuously employed in a form of labor while on this earth."[6]

Calvin took this work ethic even further by stating that God would punish workers who neglected to use their God-given gifts.[7] The General Assembly of the Presbyterian Church (USA) stated in 1995: "Hard work has marked Calvinist Christians from long ago. At their spiritual best, Calvinists have been energized to work by this security of a faith-filled ethic."[8]

However industrious the Calvinists have been since the Reformation, Calvin would not point to work as the primary focus, but to God. Dr. David Jensen, the dean of my Presbyterian seminary, states this succinctly: "The primary value of our labors is not the work itself, but the One who calls us to labor. Work is precious because God summons us to work."[9]

Spiritual Significance of Work

Calvin lived in a Christian world dominated by the Catholic belief that spiritual work, performed by monks and clerics, was superior to earthly work performed by most of the population. Following Luther's lead, he advocated that all occupations have equal value. He even went further by

---

5. Wallace, *Calvin's Doctrine of the Christian*, 155.
6. Wallace, *Calvin's Doctrine of the Christian*, 155.
7. Calvin, *Institutes of the Christian Religion*, 168.
8. *God's Work in Our Hands*, 6.
9. Jensen, *Responsive Labor*, 35.

stating that "God sets more value on the pious management of a house-hold." Serving God in a vocation is better.[10]

Calvin supported his beliefs in the spiritual significance of ordinary work using Paul's words: "Now there are varieties of gifts, but the same Spirit; and there are varieties of services, but the same Lord; and there are varieties of activities, but it is the same God who activates all of them in everyone" (1 Cor 12:4–6).

Calvin believed that for man to be obedient to God in work, he must perform work looking "to God in everything he does," and "at the same time diverted from all vain thoughts."[11] The Spirit is present when Christians serve God in their work.

Calvin's connection of human work with the spiritual life was part of the revolutionary theology bursting out of the Reformation. According to Dr. Hart: "Calvin thus confers on human work a spiritual dignity and value which it never had before. Medieval work had been an earthly duty having no immediate connection with faith and spiritual life; Calvin tied work tightly to the Christian life."[12]

For their earthly work to have meaning and purpose, Christians are called to connect their work with God's kingdom. Calvin wrote, "We ought not to live in order to eat and drink; but we must eat and drink in order to be led towards the life to come."[13]

Equal Value of All Types of Work

John Calvin strongly believed in the value of all vocations and stressed the equality of all kinds of work: "In following your proper calling, no work will be so mean and sordid as not to have a splendor and value in the eye of God.[14]

While God gives different gifts to different people, their services are to the same God. Calvin wrote:

> If a chamber-maid sweeps the floor, if a servant goes to fetch wa-ter, and they do these things well, it is not thought to be of much

10. Calvin, *Institutes of the Christian Religion*, 838.
11. Calvin, *Institutes of the Christian Religion*, 450.
12. Hart, "John Calvin," 135.
13. Wallace, *Calvin's Doctrine of the Christian*, 128.
14. Calvin, *Institutes of the Christian Religion*, 472.

importance. Nevertheless, when they do it offering themselves to God . . . such labour is accepted from them as a holy and pure oblation.[15]

Not only did Calvin confront the Catholic Church by connecting earthly toil with the spiritual life, he also aligned with Martin Luther against the prevailing belief that spiritual vocations were superior to secular vocations. Again, this was revolutionary during Calvin's time.

Self-Denial

Calvin sought to steer a balanced course for Christians on the proper use of God's abundant providence. The Catholic Church taught the spiritual virtues of self-denial through the ascetic life. Calvin dismissed this lifestyle: "Necessity, according to them, was abstinence from everything which could be wanted, so that they held it scarcely lawful to make any addition to bread and water."[16]

Calvin advocated that God's providence was a good and beautiful gift. Calvin looked to King David as a model: "You prepare a table before me in the presence of my enemies; you anoint my head with oil; my cup overflows" (Ps 23:5). He believed that life is to be enjoyed through God's generous gifts of beauty, smell, and taste.[17]

He closely followed Luther's belief that this balanced life also required self-denial of excessive abundance and possessions. Those that are "always hunting after new pleasures" are "very far from a legitimate use of the gifts of God." Humans must suppress these desires and "use the gifts of God purely with a pure conscience.[18]

It is far more dangerous to be rich than poor because "those who are much occupied with the care of the body, usually give little care to the soul."[19] Being rich through God's blessing isn't, by itself, an issue.[20] What matters is how possessions are used and the effect they have on the rich

15. Hart, "John Calvin," 128.

16. Calvin, *Institutes of the Christian Religion*, 470.

17. Calvin, *Institutes of the Christian Religion*, 470.

18. Calvin, *Institutes of the Christian Religion*, 553.

19. Calvin, *Institutes of the Christian Religion*, 471.

20. Hart, "John Calvin," 134.

person's spiritual life. Calvin believed that "we are to use its [earthly] blessings only insofar as they assist our progress, rather than retard it."[21]

Therefore, Calvin steered people toward a life of moderation. Christian work should not abuse the gifts of God. According to Calvin, even if a Christian has means to do otherwise, they should live in a "sober and frugal manner." Even though we have liberty to use this world freely our aim must be "to indulge as little as possible," curbing luxury and cutting out all show of superfluous abundance."[22] Human work is the use of God's gifts in moderation to provide for our earthly existence. To be obedient to God in work is to live a balanced and moderate life, enjoying God's gifts with thankfulness, without excesses or abuses. Calvin wrote: "We must learn to be no less placid and patient in enduring penury, than moderate in enjoying abundance."[23] Obedience begins with a humble attitude based on Luke's Gospel: "For all who exalt themselves will be humbled, and those who humble themselves will be exalted" (Luke 14:11).

Service to Others

Calvin believed in Christian community mutually benefiting from their diverse collection of God-given talents. Although the concept of the economic division of labor had not yet been expressed as such, Calvin applied this to his theology of work. He believed in serving the community and being served by the community. He shared Luther's view that God limited each worker to one vocation and believed this encouraged interdependence: "This is as God intended."[24]

Calvin used Genesis again as the basis of his theology: "So God created humankind in his image, in the image of God he created them" (Gen 1:27).

Dr. Wallace wrote:

> These two basic facts—that all men are created in the image of God, and that all share in a common human nature—are the foundation of all Calvin's teaching about human relationships.

---

21. Calvin, *Institutes of the Christian Religion*, 469.

22. Wallace, *Calvin's Doctrine of the Christian*, 176.

23. Calvin, *Institutes of the Christian Religion*, 471.

24. Hart, "John Calvin," 126.

They themselves define the "order of nature" according to which a Christian, as well as any other man, must live.[25]

Calvin then linked self-denial with service to our neighbors. Wealth gained through industrious work is to be used in service to others. Through giving, we balance our own self-centered tendencies.[26] When people are blessed with abundance, instead of accumulating possessions with clenched hands, Calvin's theology called for workers with abundance to unclench their hands and share. "Whoever be the man that is presented to you as needing your assistance, you have no ground for declining to give it to him."[27] Calvin taught that obedience to God in human work required sharing our abundance by serving our neighbors.

Business Ethics

Following Luther's lead, Calvin's theology of work included specific Christian behaviors related to business ethics. It is noteworthy that many of Calvin's teachings are still relevant to current business practices. According to Timothy J. Keller, a Presbyterian pastor who wrote *Every Good Endeavor: Connecting Your Work to God's Work,*

> Christianity gives us very specific teachings about human nature and what makes human beings flourish. We must ensure that our work is done in line with these understandings. Faithful work, then, is to operate out of a Christian "worldview."[28]

Here are a few examples of Calvin's business ethics.

First, just as God is the loving master of humankind, employers must treat their employees and community with love and fairness. Calvin writes:

> I am the master, but not in a tyrannical way; I am the master, but on condition that I am also a brother; I am the master, but there is a common master in heaven for both me and those who are under me; we are all in one family.[29]

---

25. Wallace, *Calvin's Doctrine of the Christian,* 150.
26. Wallace, *Calvin's Doctrine of the Christian,* 185–86.
27. Calvin, *Institutes of the Christian Religion,* 453.
28. Keller, *Every Good Endeavor,* 4–5.
29. Hart, "John Calvin," 131.

Christian community, based on loving God and neighbor as reflected in Jesus' words in the Gospel of Luke (Luke 10:27), was central to Calvin's theology of work. Obedience to God in the workplace is treating employees fairly.

Second, employees should respect their employers. Leaders should be honored and esteemed for the office they occupy.[30] While being respectful, employees are not to blindly follow their employer or ruler, but be ruled only by God's law.[31]

Third, unlike Luther, Calvin did not negatively view earned profits, for Calvin believed that humans should be rewarded for their hard work and good business management skills.[32] As stated previously, what was foundational in Calvin's theology of work was the way people viewed their possessions and whether they shared them with their neighbors. Dr. Jensen agrees: "Work, as vocation, is fulfilling not because it enriches oneself (though it may), but because of its obedient response to the creator."[33] Obedience to God is also earning income for the good of the community, as Calvin stated when preaching on Ephesians 4:28 ("Thieves must give up stealing; rather let them labor and work honestly with their own hands, so as to have something to share with the needy."). The community must benefit from our labor.[34]

Fourth, unlike Luther, Calvin positively viewed trade and commerce as benefiting and uniting the community: "The import and export of goods brings no small advantage to men. And especially since God desires the whole human race to be united in mutual service, it is impossible to disapprove."[35] This issue continues to be debated.

Finally, Calvin addressed legal action and differed with Luther. Calvin insisted that it is correct for Christians to resort to civil authorities to have wrongs put right. Preserving a community of love is balanced through civil justice which preserves the community and punishes those that abuse.[36]

We are all products of our time and place in history. Calvin's systematic theology sought to return Christianity to a religion based on Scripture

30. Calvin, *Institutes of the Christian Religion*, 983.

31. Calvin, *Institutes of the Christian Religion*, 988.

32. Hart, "John Calvin," 133.

33. Jensen, *Responsive Labor*, 36.

34. Volf, *Work in the Spirit*, 189.

35. Hart, "John Calvin," 133.

36. Calvin, *Institutes of the Christian Religion*, 982.

rather than traditions accumulated over more than a thousand years of Christendom. His theology was fundamental to the emerging Protestant movement and countered the more powerful Catholic Church. Calvin's theology understandably stressed the need to equalize all vocations, given the church's deviation from Scripture on numerous theological issues. Scripture clearly highlights that God created humanity with many talents, but all are joined together in the same Spirit. All Christians, with their diverse gifts, are to labor together always looking to God—our Creator, Redeemer, and Sustainer. This concept was Calvin's greatest contribution to the theology of work.

I find Calvin's work theology more balanced than the ensuing Protestant work ethic. I cannot find any sources where Calvin placed work above spiritual matters. He stressed moderation; work was primarily to provide for our earthly existence. Calvin strongly believed that Christian humility was required during the pursuit of a spiritual life praising God. Boasting of individual works was idolatrous. It is true that Calvin wanted Christians to be productive with their time and talents, as God's gifts were not to be wasted. But Calvin's productive work theology has been stretched over time so it no longer allows rest for a spiritual life—something Calvin would vehemently oppose.

After the Puritan period of the fifteenth and sixteenth centuries, when theologians such as William Perkins (1558–1602) wrote detailed treatises on the Doctrine of Vocations, Western Christianity slowly deviated from these beliefs. Liberal theology, which emphasized the use of reason, science, freedom, and experience, while focusing on human goodness and progress, became the Protestant theological norm during the Enlightenment period (1685–1815). It was more than 300 years after John Calvin before a Protestant theologian would revert work theology back to its Reformation foundations. This reversion happened with the hindsight of the Industrial Revolution, liberal theology, and two world wars. His name was Dr. Karl Barth, considered the greatest twentieth-century Protestant theologian.

In summary, John Calvin:

- Founded his theology of work on God's Genesis curse on work which was tempered by God's graciousness.

- Believed in hard, industrial work (Protestant work ethic) and that it is sinful to waste our gifts through idleness (agreed with Luther).

- Connected human work with the spiritual life that was tightly tied to the Christian life.

- Believed in the value of all vocations (agreed with Luther).

- Supported a balanced course for Christians: advocated God's bountiful providence with modest behavior.

- Advocated community service to others (agreed with Luther).

- Followed Luther's lead in recommending specific business ethics but differed on such issues as trade and civil justice.

Beyond Christendom (1775–present)

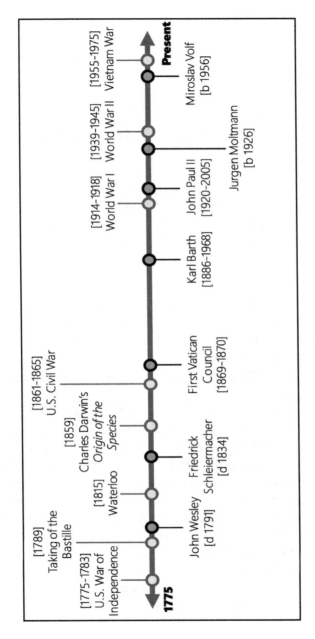

Figure 7—Beyond Christendom Timeline

Karl Barth (1886–1968)— The Neo-Orthodoxy Theologian

Can man view and tackle his own work under the command of God without first, as the same command of God enjoins, pausing, resting and keeping holy-day in the sight of God, rejoicing in freedom?[1]

KARL BARTH WAS BORN into a theological family in Basel, Switzerland. He started his career as a village Reformed pastor and later taught theology in Germany and Switzerland. He witnessed two world wars, which profoundly influenced his theology and led him to reject the liberal theology of his predecessors. Barth was a leader of the theological movement named neo-orthodoxy that opposed liberal theology and stressed Reformation themes such as the centrality of Christ. Many consider Barth the leading theologian of the twentieth century. He gained the attention of the mainstream public when he was featured on the cover of *Time* in 1962.

Barth is a difficult read, even for students of theology, and especially for persons trained to think and write concisely. I initially encountered his writings during my first semester of seminary. My theology professor was a Barthian expert, and she included in the class readings several sections of his systematic theology seminal works, *Church Dogmatics*. His fourteen-volume theological masterpiece has 6 million words and 8,000 pages, English translated from German—and he didn't even complete the series! Thankfully, our class was told to skip the lengthy footnotes that could run for pages. I struggled with his writings, as he verbosely rephrased concepts

1. Barth, *Doctrine of Creation*, 3:51.

until my brain went to mush. In addition, my theological vocabulary was limited, as I did not know Greek or Latin, which he frequently used.

During my second semester, when I knew I wasn't going to escape him, I intensely studied Barth's theological writings. What a surprise when, after a few weeks, Barth's theological views started to resonate with me. I just wished he could have communicated them better to the masses. My connection with Barth may have grown out of his neo-orthodoxy theology, since it tied back to the Reformation and John Calvin.

Theology of Work

The theology of Karl Barth centers on the Gospel of Jesus Christ. He wrote, "Theology must begin with Jesus Christ, and not with general principles . . . Theology must also end with Him, and not with supposedly self-evident general conclusions."[2] Barth disagreed with the liberal theologians who supported natural theology, which Barth defined as "the doctrine of a union of man with God existing outside God's revelation in Jesus Christ."[3] Barth agreed that a historical understanding of Scripture has a place within the church, but he devalued historical theology as the primary means of biblical interpretation and shifted to dialectical theology that stressed the paradoxical nature of divine truth. An example of dialectical theology is two opposing truths: God condemns humans for their sinfulness and also freely offers mercy. Barth wrote:

> When religion becomes conscious of religion, when it becomes a psychologically and historically conceivable magnitude in the world, it falls away from its inner character, from its truth, to idols. Its truth is its other-worldliness, its refusal of the idea of sacredness, its non-historicity.[4]

For Barth, Scripture pointed to Jesus Christ, who is the Word: "The Christian community does not exist for itself; it exists for the Gospel."[5] The running joke during my seminary study of Barth was that if you fell asleep during class and the professor asked you a question about Barth, you should just answer "Jesus Christ!" and you'd always be right.

2. Barth, *Selection*, 87–88.

3. Barth, *Selection*, 51.

4. Barth, *Word of God*, 68–69.

5. Barth, *Selection*, 66.

Calvin and Barth published their theological views about 400 years apart. Both theologians approached the theology of work through Genesis but used different Scriptures. Calvin based his theology around Genesis 3:17–19, and believed that "God had made man to work,"[6] which is known as the Protestant work ethic. Barth approached the theology of work through the Sabbath (Gen 2:2–3), the day of rest. British theologian Dr. Philip West wrote on Barth: "Work does have some place in the divine plan, but its place is on the circumference rather than in the centre of the divine plan and action."[7] These two theological approaches have divergent implications for working Christians who want to be obedient to God.

Sabbath

While the theology of Karl Barth centers on the Gospel of Jesus Christ, Barth begins his theology of work using Genesis and God's Holy Day:

> And on the seventh day God finished the work that he had done, and he rested on the seventh day from all the work that he had done. So God blessed the seventh day and hallowed it, because on it God rested from all the work that he had done in creation. (Gen 2:2–3)

What does the Sabbath have to do with the theology of work? Barth's theological premise was that rest was above work. When humans cease working on the Sabbath, the focus is not on human works, but on God.[8] Humankind was created on the sixth day and, on the first day after their creation, they rested with God instead of working:

> On this day the creature, too, is to have a "breathing space" in consequence of and in accordance with the fact that God the Creator also rested on the seventh day of creation, celebrating, rejoicing, and in freedom establishing His special lordship over the finished creation.[9]

Theology professor Darrell Cosden writes that Barth "addressed work within protology [referring to the study of the beginning of the world], but

---

6. Hart, "John Calvin," 121.
7. West, "Karl Barth's Theology of Work," 16.
8. Barth, *Doctrine of Creation*, 3:50.
9. Barth, *Doctrine of Creation*, 3:52.

rather than starting with a calling to human activity he took the Sabbath to be the logical and conceptual theological starting point."[10]

Barth then linked the Holy Day to the New Testament, which celebrates Christ's resurrection on the first day of the week. "On the first day of the week, when we met to break bread, Paul was holding a discussion with them" (Acts 20:7). This is the "Lord's Day," to be kept as holy. This is the day of rest which God commanded.[11] Resting with God comes before work, says Barth. Dr. West wrote:

> He attacks the pervasive idea that rest or recreation gains its primary significance from work, the idea that the only real meaning to be attached to rest is its ability to enable us to work more efficiently afterwards. This, Barth says, is to define rest in terms of work rather than work in terms of rest—a fundamental mistake that the symbol of the sabbath stands against.[12]

By reflecting on the Sabbath commandment and the Lord's Day, Cosden writes that the "sabbath becomes paradigmatic and is meant to be a principle that permeates and transforms the entire nature and structure of work ... Work is not the opposite of sabbath, but rather, that sabbath rest should be a characteristic of all human activity and thus also of work."[13] As Associate Professor of Theological Ethics at the University of Exeter, Ester D. Reed writes, "The Sabbath teaches *freedom from* the seeming ultimacy of earthly work and its related concerns, and *freedom for* both self and God."[14] The day of rest is more important than the days of work. This was Barth's greatest contribution to the theology of work. The Sabbath comes first in priority.

Human Work is Not Divine

Barth viewed creation as God's activity and rejected a theology of work that identified humans as co-creative. Humans were not around when God created the world. "Man was never the witness of any of it, but was himself only its final object."[15] There is no connection between God's creative

---

10. Cosden, *Theology of Work*, 45.

11. Barth, *Doctrine of Creation*, 3:53.

12. West, "Karl Barth's Theology of Work," 13.

13. Cosden, *Theology of Work*, 45.

14. Reed, *Work, for God's Sake*, 104 (emphasis hers).

15. Barth, *Doctrine of Creation*, 3:52.

activity and human work. God did not need humans to create the world.[16] Barth viewed human work as earthly toil and vastly subservient to God's work of creation:

> Man does not do anything special by working. He has no reason to congratulate himself that he is not lazy. Work does not make him a second God . . . We cannot classify human work as a divine act. For it is not really a creation but a movement within the created world . . . It would be highly arrogant and materially more than doubtful to maintain that God's work is improved or adorned by human labour.[17]

Rejection of the Protestant Work Ethic

While John Calvin wrote his systematic theology setting the foundation of the Protestant work ethic, Barth had the advantage of living 400 years later in time. Barth saw the Industrial Age abuses that enslaved people to their work and left them spiritually void. Barth's Neo-orthodoxy theology stressed the need, after many years of liberal theology, to return to Scripture and theologically reflect on fundamental topics such as work. Barth wrote, "The practical requirements, the ideals and even perhaps the myth of modern Western civilization with its ethos of work are a very different thing from the command of God."[18] Barth built his work theology with a scriptural foundation starting with Jesus Christ's work as a carpenter. He acknowledges that Jesus worked but his occupation was a minor part of the gospel. "On the contrary, He seems to have summoned His disciples away from their secular work."[19] The same is true for Paul who had little to say on work or his earthly achievements. Barth wrote, "We search both his own writings and the rest of the New Testament in vain for the passion with which the "Subdue the earth" of Gen. 1:28 has been interpreted and applied since the 16th century."[20]

Barth also found a similar lower priority for work searching Old Testament Scripture:

16. West, "Karl Barth's Theology of Work," 15.

17. Barth, *Doctrine of Creation*, 3:520.

18. Barth, *Doctrine of Creation*, 3:472.

19. Barth, *Doctrine of Creation*, 3:472.

20. Barth, *Doctrine of Creation*, 3:472.

The same is true of the Old Testament. We are surely reading into the saying in Gen. 1:28 more than is actually there if we take it to imply that cultivation is the real task which the Creator has set man; and the same applies to the observation in Gen. 2:15 that God put man in the Garden of Eden "to dress and to keep it."[21]

Work is necessary to sustain life and is supported by Scripture, wrote Barth, citing Psalm 104:23, "People go out to their work and to their labor until the evening." So if work was a priority, why did God not command it as a weekday activity? Yet, God did command the Sabbath.[22] Barth concluded his scriptural review by questioning the priority of the Protestant work ethic in relation to resting in God. He firmly believed that work has a lower priority in importance, "very much in the background, if not completely invisible."[23] Australian New Testament scholar Dr. Robert J. Banks writes:

> Though work is necessary, it is peripheral to God's central work of reconciliation. It is only a part of "the active life" Christians are called to lead, a part that is subordinate to prayer, witness, and service.[24]

Christians must guard against prioritizing work too highly, as they may fall into the trap of placing work above faith. Justifying self-worth through human work or boasting of work accomplishments goes directly against Scripture: "Let the one who boasts, boast in the Lord" (1 Cor 1:31).

Criteria for Work—Prolonging Life

If work is secondary and not a central objective for humans, what are the criteria for being obedient to God in human work? First, work prolongs life on earth and is a necessary part of life. Barth wrote:

> Man must work to live. For the sake of his inner and outer independence, he is required not to busy himself in useless matters but to care for his life. Nor is he to live as an unlawful recipient, but as a free giver. It is for these reasons that the work of his hands is demanded.[25]

21. Barth, *Doctrine of Creation*, 3:472.
22. Barth, *Doctrine of Creation*, 3:473.
23. Barth, *Doctrine of Creation*, 3:472.
24. Banks, *Faith Goes to Work*, 165.
25. Barth, *Doctrine of Creation*, 3:526.

To be obedient to God, according to Barth, means being at the disposal of God and that means remaining alive: "For no one can obey God without willing to be man and therefore without pulling himself together, without turning with whole-hearted loyalty to the earthly and creaturely work of this synthesis, and therefore without being prepared to work."[26]

Barth agreed with Calvin that humans should work. However, Barth placed the boundaries of work activity around the activities that prolong life: "What is basically at issue in all fields of human work is the desire of men to 'prolong' their own lives and those of their relatives . . . to earn their daily bread and a little more."[27] To obey God is to work to prolong human life, as how would humans survive without the basic human needs obtained through work? Catholic theologian Edwin G. Kaiser wrote: "Karl Barth characterized food or substance as the purposive determinant underlying all work, the basic motivation of all work, and considers it essential to work that man be prepared to do himself what is possible in order to guarantee his own existence."[28]

Caring for Humanity

Since work is intended to prolong life, Barth viewed an individual's struggle for earthly existence within the greater context of community and advocated cooperation instead of competition. He wrote, "Human work can and should take place in co-existence and co-operation."[29] He supported his view using Scripture: "Do not seek your own advantage, but that of the other" (1 Cor 10:24) and "Bear one another's burdens, and in this way you will fulfill the law of Christ" (Gal 6:2). The Presbyterian Church (USA) affirms Barth's theology:

> By God's intention, we live not in isolation but in community. Our work reminds us that we need one another. That without participation in each other's lives, we would not be human.[30]

First, according to Barth, humans must understand that all workers have the same goal of prolonging life. Thus, humans must allow all to earn their

26. Barth, *Doctrine of Creation*, 3:523.

27. Barth, *Doctrine of Creation*, 3:525.

28. Kaiser, *Theology of Work*, 59.

29. Barth, *Doctrine of Creation*, 3:536.

30. *God's Work in our Hands*, 14.

livelihood: "Work is a social act involving association and comradeship."[31] Second, human work is not a game, since winning denies life to the losing competitors. "There is no fun in this contest."[32] Obedience to God in work means caring for humanity by allowing all workers to share in God's providence through cooperation. The Henry B. Wright Professor of Theology at Yale University, Dr. Miroslav Volf, wrote that Barth "rightly maintained that true humanity is realized only when people live with one another in such a way that they do not live against one another or simply next to one another, but *for* one another."[33]

Self-Denial

Barth lived during the rapid rise of capitalism and he witnessed the negatives of economic competition, writing, "It can hardly be denied that on the whole, at least in the West, the modern industrial process does in fact rest on the principle of the exploitation of some by others."[34]

While Calvin steered a course for moderation, Barth advocated socialism that placed boundaries on competition, rather than capitalism or communism.[35] Obedience to God in human work means self-denial "and therefore a call for the championing of the weak against every kind of encroachment on the part of the strong."[36]

Service to Others

Like his predecessors Luther and Calvin, community was central to Barth and obedience to God includes community service.[37] Barth again turned to Scripture to support work as service to others:

- "Then once more you shall see the difference between the righteous and the wicked, between one who serves God and one who does not serve him" (Mal 3:18).

31. Barth, *Doctrine of Creation*, 3:537.
32. Barth, *Doctrine of Creation*, 3:540.
33. Volf, *Work in the Spirit*, 191 (emphasis his).
34. Barth, *Doctrine of Creation*, 3:542.
35. Barth, *Doctrine of Creation*, 3:538.
36. Barth, *Doctrine of Creation*, 3:544.
37. Barth, *Doctrine of Creation*, 3:474–75.

- "No one can serve two masters; for a slave will either hate the one and love the other, or be devoted to the one and despise the other. You cannot serve God and wealth" (Matt 6:24).

Christology was always central to Barth's theology and to his criteria that work must be of service to humanity. He wrote, "He can be obedient to God only as he follows Jesus Christ, so that in his place and within his limits he with his action is the witness of Jesus Christ and therefore of God's will and work."[38] Humans must look to Christ as the best example of how God wants humanity to act while on earth. Christ came to serve others. "In Christ, the truly human one," writes Robert Banks, "we find criteria for truly human work, work which is an analogy to the personal relationship between Father and Son in the Trinity."[39] Obedience to God is to be a witness to Christ in service to others. Caring for our fellow creatures exhibits the kingdom of God.[40]

Business Ethics

Unlike Luther and Calvin, Barth did not offer many specifics on business ethics:

> The decisive task of Christian ethics is not to discover and assess such universal categories but to establish the fact that always, everywhere and in all circumstances a boundary has been drawn in this respect, too, between work which is commanded and legitimate and work which is forbidden and illegitimate . . . Thus, at a specific time and in a specific situation Christian ethics is forced to look in a specific direction on both sides.[41]

Barth maintains a high-level theology on ethics since he believes that ethical questions must be addressed for a certain time and place.

Barth did offer a few specifics, though. He was against capitalism on the grounds that it exploited workers and determined winners while losers faced extinction. He was also against communism, which removed freedom from workers, enriched the few powerful leaders, and stifled religious

38. Barth, *Doctrine of Creation*, 3:482.
39. Banks, *Faith Goes to Work*, 165.
40. Barth, *Doctrine of Creation*, 3:503.
41. Barth, *Doctrine of Creation*, 3:534.

freedom.[42] West says, "Both [New Right and Marxist left] . . . share an assumption about the centrality of labour in human life, an assumption that Barth's account usefully challenges."[43] Barth gives a general rule on business ethics based on his first criteria for work—the prolongation of life. Serving human existence is "honest" work.[44]

Barth sought to rectify the problems arising from the Protestant work ethic in his theology of work. He had the benefit of history having experienced tragic historical events such as two world wars and the resulting aftermath of the Cold War. Like Luther and Calvin in many ways, Barth's primary goal was to return the church to its scriptural roots centered in Jesus Christ and away from liberal theology centered on enlightened reason. Barth was pessimistic about the ability of humans to progress without looking first to Christ as their model.

No Linkage of Work and Spirit

Both Calvin and Barth believed that work was primarily to prolong the earthly life, both for the individual and humanity. However, Calvin emphasized the spiritual significance of work much more than Barth. Luther divided the world into two kingdoms: God's (spiritual) and the temporal. A Christian's work life was connected to his or her spiritual life. Barth did not deny that work was part of the active Christian life, but placed it on the periphery. In fact, Barth did not link work and Spirit in his writings, although his writings placed work among the tasks of the active Christian life. By focusing on work as a means to prolong life and by challenging the Protestant work ethic through the prioritization of rest, he theologically steered too far away from the spiritual aspect of work. While Barth's criteria for work does allow the Spirit to be present during labor, he should have prioritized the spiritual qualities of work to a greater extent. As Calvin emphasized, God's gifts and the Spirit can be united. My opinion is that even if the world had an economic system that equally distributed all of God's providence, humans would still engage their individual talents in work that filled the majority of their weekdays to prolong life. Christians want reassurance that their work has more than utilitarian meaning, as well as a balanced life that allows for rest during the Sabbath.

42. Barth, *Doctrine of Creation*, 3:532.
43. West, "Karl Barth's Theology of Work," 18.
44. Barth, *Doctrine of Creation*, 3:530.

The post-Barth world has not heeded his call for resting in God while placing work on the circumference. Work, for most Christians, is central to their lives. The competition to survive continues at an accelerating rate as the global economy has turned more capitalistic since the downfall of communism. The gap increases between the wealthy and the poor. For the majority of Americans, the Lord's Day is not a day of resting in God, but has slowly become a day like the other six days of the week. Burnout and depression are widespread, as is substance abuse in order to cope with a meaningless life. Craving space has edged out creating time for the eternal. This leads us back to Germany and another theologian with hope, Jürgen Moltmann.

In summary, Barth:

- Centered his theology of work around the Sabbath; resting in God comes before work.
- Rejected the liberal theology of work that identified humans as "co-creative" with God.
- Rejected the Protestant work ethic by showing work as a lower priority in Scripture.
- Believed that the main criteria for work is to prolong life.
- Supported socialism ("self-denial") over capitalism and communism.
- Agreed with both Luther and Calvin on the importance of work in caring for our community; Christ came to serve.
- Believed that ethics should be addressed for certain times and places, but did not offer specifics.
- Rejected competition and advocated cooperation.
- Steered away from emphasizing Calvin's spiritual qualities of work.

Jürgen Moltmann (born 1926)—
Theology of Hope

The theologian is not concerned merely to supply a different *interpretation* of the world, of history and of human nature, but to *transform* them in expectation of a divine transformation.[1]

JÜRGEN MOLTMANN WAS BORN forty years after Karl Barth. He grew up in Germany in a secular home and was initially fascinated with math and physics. Like Barth, he lived through World War II. But unlike Barth, he was drafted into the German army and sent to the front lines. He surrendered to the British in 1945 and was a prisoner of war until his release in 1948. During his time in prison, an American chaplain gave him a copy of the New Testament and the Psalms. After reading them, he became a Christian. In the midst of terrible suffering and a devastated Europe, Moltmann found hope in the risen Christ. He graduated with a doctorate in theology from the University of Göttingen, the university where Barth taught before the Second World War, and eventually became professor of systematic theology at the University of Tübingen. Moltmann focused on eschatology, the study of the things to come, and his most famous publication was *Theology of Hope*. He said, "I wanted to build up the doctrine of creation from the new creation of heaven and earth (from Rev 21) not, as is usual, from creation-in-the-beginning (that is, in the light of Gen 1)."[2]

Moltmann's contribution to the theology of work was found primarily in his 1984 publication *On Human Dignity: Political Theology and Ethics,*

1. Moltmann, *Theology of Hope*, 84.
2. Moltmann, *Theology of Hope*, 11.

a collection of theological essays. Chapter 3, "The Right to Meaningful Work," contains the bulk of his theological beliefs on work. This chapter is packed with insightful theology, some that aligns and some that differs with Barth's theology of work.

Meaningful Work is a Human Right

Moltmann wrote his theology as part of his beliefs on human rights and dignity. It is based on the St. Pölten Report, a 1974 ecumenical consultation held in St. Pölten, Austria, by the Commission of the Churches on International Affairs (CCIA) of the World Council of Churches. One of the features of the report is that work is a human right.[3] He extended his argument further by stating the types of work included in human rights: "The *right to work* is not a demand for just any kind of work but for humane work, work that is meaningful for human beings."[4] He agreed with Barth that humans needed to work to sustain life, but unlike Barth, he believed work was more than just about sustaining life. Work must have meaning which includes self-actualization. "Work instills in a person feelings of independence and ability and thus self-consciousness. Every unemployed person knows that."[5]

Sabbath

Barth centered his theology on Sabbath rest. Humans resting in God came before work, both in biblical order and in their hierarchy of importance. Moltmann agreed with this biblical ordering: "Although the sabbath of creation was the seventh day for God, for the human beings who were created on the sixth day, it was the first day they experienced."[6] He certainly agreed that the Sabbath is important: "Human beings are the last to be created before the sabbath, and are created for that."[7] But he did not place human work below the Sabbath rest. He places the work day and the Sabbath as

---

3. Moltmann, *On Human Dignity*, 6.

4. Moltmann, *On Human Dignity*, 37 (emphasis his).

5. Moltmann, *On Human Dignity*, 53–54.

6. Moltmann, *God in Creation*, 295.

7. Moltmann, *God in Creation*, 228.

equals with work "defined through the Sabbath."[8] Therefore, Moltmann saw the Sabbath and work as complementary human responses to God.

Work Has Existence Value

Moltmann elevated work above its simple production value to support our physical needs; work has *existence value*. This is a major break from Barth. Work must be more than an economic production value, but full of joy and playfulness. Yes, human work needs to be useful to society and have a serious purpose. But in addition, workers understand themselves through their work. As Moltmann once wrote, "In the seriousness of work also belongs, in a human sense, the relaxed joy of existence: Let it be!"[9]

Theology of Play

Moltmann expanded on his "freedom for self-presentation and thus playfulness" statement in his earlier (1972) publication, *Theology of Play*:

> To be happy, to enjoy ourselves, we must above all be free . . . We enjoy ourselves, we laugh, when our burdens are removed, when fetters are falling, pressures yield and obstructions give way. Then our hearts leap within us and we suddenly find it easy to cope with other men and circumstances. We gain distance from ourselves and our plans move forward in a natural, unforced way.[10]

He gave a short history as to how humans have moved back and forth between fighting for freedoms and then losing those newfound freedoms. During the Reformation, the Protestants battled Catholics over theological issues such as faith versus works. The Protestant Reformers established piety which precluded entertainment and fun activities. Then the Puritans stressed industrialization and frugality "among the very people who had at first insisted on believing that men are justified by faith alone." In Eastern Europe, communism shut down the social gathering places (coffee houses, restaurants, etc.), "the very ones in which the revolution itself had once been debated and plotted."[11] Moltmann advocates playing games, which

8. Moltmann, *On Human Dignity*, 41.

9. Moltmann, *On Human Dignity*, 41.

10. Moltmann, *Theology of Play*, 1.

11. Moltmann, *Theology of Play*, 10–11.

allows for freedom that liberates society: "We discover with a laugh that things need not at all be as they are and as we have been told they have to be. When the fetters are suddenly removed, we try to walk upright.[12]

At the core of liberation and freedom through play is the belief that work does not define humans. Human existence is not determined by our work, be it a success or a failure. Joy was already there before work as we started from leisure.[13]

> No one *has* to justify himself through work. No one *has* to demonstrate her right to existence through work! No one *has* to realize himself through work. Were that true, then the unemployed would have no rights and the handicapped no reality.[14]

Moltmann fully agreed with Barth that work did not define the existence of humans. We were all first loved by God and created in God's image. A person is not free if work defines him or her. This makes humans dependent on their work and subject to the work. "So works do not make the person, but a person does works. And the person is made by God. A person receives himself from God."[15]

During this play at work, human creativity and expression allow workers to be self-representative. What humans create is "an expression of the *demonstrative value of being*." Our being is expressed through the creative process of work. Moltmann then separates self-representation from self-realization. He defines self-representation as "endless beauties and liberties of the finite concomitants of the infinite joy of the creator" while self-realization results in "successes and accomplishments."[16]

Although Moltmann was clear that creative play was not dependent on accomplishments, play does achieve identity or self-realization. "Creative work is self-realization, achievement of individual identity: I am, because I work. I am what I make of myself." [17] He later backed off from using self-realization because it threatens those persons who might not be able to work, such as the aged, unemployed, or handicapped.[18] Moltmann felt

---

12. Moltmann, *Theology of Play*, 12–13.

13. Moltmann, *Theology of Play*, 21.

14. Moltmann, *On Human Dignity*, 54 (emphasis his).

15. Moltmann, *Theology of Play*, 46–47.

16. Moltmann, *Theology of Play*, 22–23 (emphasis his).

17. Moltmann, *On Human Dignity*, 50–51.

18. Moltmann, *On Human Dignity*, 54.

uncomfortable with any term that focused on outcomes except for creative self-expression.

When I first read Moltmann's *Theology of Play*, I found it unrealistic and naive. On my second reading, I found some merit in his ideas, but his arguments seemed skewed. Even a tenured university professor does work that is not creative play. Sitting in dull meetings, dealing with difficult students, and attending university fundraisers likely do not qualify as creative play. Moltmann's *Theology of Play* is powerful when he confronts work that does not allow some expression of creativity and treats workers as mere unthinking objects to achieve solely utilitarian purposes. In today's economy, creativity is valued and desired. Organizations that are not creative and do not allow people to achieve individual creative expression will not survive for long. Certainly, there are limits to creativity and self-realization. Balance is required and equilibrium depends on the occupation. I want my doctor to be creative in diagnosing my illness, yet I also want him or her to apply proven treatments that might be boring and repetitive to implement. Too much play might endanger my life or the existence of the organization for which I work.

Cosden's Critique of Moltmann

My comments are supported by Darrell Cosden, a retired professor of theological studies at Judson University, a conservative Baptist liberal arts college located in Elgin, Illinois. He earned his PhD in theology from the University of St. Andrews in Scotland, and later published his dissertation in a theological monograph titled *A Theology of Work*. Much of his book is devoted to a thorough outline of Moltmann's books and a dissection of Moltmann's theology of work. Cosden praises Moltmann, saying that he "has done theology a great service by pointing toward and offering an understanding of work which highlights its meaning for the whole of life and not only for the person and society."[19]

Cosden also *critiques* Moltmann. On guaranteeing meaningful work, Cosden parallels my concerns. He also desires that human work be meaningful and creative. But economic realities of supply and demand must be considered as serious forces in society.[20] Guaranteeing workers the right to creative and playful work "may be a good social goal to move toward. How-

19. Cosden, *Theology of Work*, 77.
20. Cosden, *Theology of Work*, 63.

ever, if this goal is not then taken in relation to other social goals and social realities (for example, economic realities) then the goal itself becomes so abstract that it becomes useless for practical ethical purposes."[21] Cosden suggests "that any theology of work, or theological construal of work, needs to be able to equally take account of economics as a discipline (this however, does not mean capitulate to the discipline)."[22] This was refreshing to read given my professional experience in business and finance.

Cosden critiques Moltmann's fear of self-realization and believes Moltmann's fear is due to "equating self-realization with justification." Cosden disagrees with this assumption. He believes that through a person's work, they change and become something new through the process. People "realize themselves in and through their work." But Moltmann resists this theologically because he fears justification by works, something that Reformed Christians preach against. Cosden believes that "people can still learn and grow in areas of their lives even if we want to affirm that they ultimately still need to experience God's justification and salvation for their whole life.[23]

Christ's Work on the Cross

Moltmann was always looking forward (eschatologically) to the new creation. This is the point where he went far beyond Barth and pointed to Christ's work on the cross. He points to the servanthood of God in Philippians 2:6–11 as the model for work. "*Work* becomes the embodiment of the doctrine of salvation . . . Through God's work people are freed from sin."[24] I never thought of Christ's sacrificial actions as being the foundations of a theology of work since God's work differs from human work. Following Augustine, Moltmann turned to the apostle Paul for an example of salvation work. Paul's apostolic activity was work:

> In 2 Cor. 11:23–28, he holds up to his opponents the fact that he has "worked more" than all others and counts as his "work"—labors, imprisonment, beatings, mortal danger, persecution, slander, hunger, thirst, cold, nakedness, and constant concern about the congregation, which he describes as follows in Gal. 4:11: "I am

21. Cosden, *Theology of Work*, 73.

22. Cosden, *Theology of Work*, 71.

23. Cosden, *Theology of Work*, 74–75.

24. Moltmann, *On Human Dignity*, 42 (emphasis his).

afraid I have labored over you in vain." The apostles are "fellow workers for the kingdom of God" (Col. 4:11).[25]

Barth's theology placed Jesus Christ at the center, but his work theology focused on Genesis. Barth was careful not to mix divine and human work. Moltmann's theology was also Christ-centered, but he linked human work to Christ's suffering and resurrection. He extends the meaning of human work to "participation in the mission and self-dedication of Jesus Christ for the kingdom of God and the freedom of humanity."[26] Moltmann infused his theology of hope into work, writing, "Man does not gain himself by distinguishing himself from 'the world,' but by emptying himself into it."[27]

Community

Like Barth, Moltmann believed strongly in community. His theology on eschatology and work as Christlike servanthood was linked to his belief that work should uplift the community toward becoming the kingdom of God.[28] He again focused on Paul and the new creation to define community "as an event from which there arises a new creation and new life."[29] For Moltmann, community did not stop with humans. He viewed community as encompassing all of God's creation.[30] Unemployment also deprives a person of community. "Through work a person gains companions, colleagues, and friends. Unemployment threatens a person with the loss of this community and with social death."[31]

Given Moltmann's view that work was a fundamental human right, he advocated that all people who are able and desiring work should be employed, whether or not they were contributing to society in a utilitarian way, because work contributed to self-expression. This was much easier stated than achieved in reality. When work is automatically given to all and guaranteed, then individuals may (and usually do in my experience) view work as entitlement, creating societal problems such as poor performance

25. Moltmann, *On Human Dignity*, 43.
26. Moltmann, *On Human Dignity*, 44.
27. Moltmann, *Theology of Hope*, 92.
28. Moltmann, *On Human Dignity*, 52.
29. Moltmann, *Theology of Hope*, 205.
30. Moltmann, *God in Creation*, 266.
31. Moltmann, *On Human Dignity*, 55.

and lack of focus. If work is guaranteed, it must be carefully enacted and provide incentives for workers to be creative, productive, and communal. In reality, government actions often steer either toward socialism with employment protection laws that tend to damage the economy, or capitalism that allows unemployment and its associated suffering.

New Creation

Moltmann concluded his theology of work by recognizing that the new creation was not yet here—humans have much work still to do. He wrote:

> The world is not finished. Through their work, people take part in the destruction or the preservation of the world. They serve not only with the creating God; they also work together with the redeeming God.[32]

And he issues a stern warning related to our current industrialized trends. He believes that industrialization means less need for manual labor, thus more unemployment. A society built upon human justification through work will be impossible to maintain. People will consider their lives as meaningless and useless. "The man who has been raised by the motto that work alone makes life enjoyable is going to be in for a very rough time."[33]

This is even more true today than in 1972, when Moltmann wrote these words. Like Barth, Moltmann is a product of industrialization and devastation. Unlike Barth, he gives more meaning to work than merely prolonging life. Barth starts with Genesis. Moltmann looks forward to the future—the new creation. This is an important development in the theology of work.

A Croatian doctoral student of Moltmann, Miroslav Volf, embraced Moltmann's eschatology focus and made it Spirit-filled for our modern culture.

In summary, Moltmann:

- Based his theology of work on human rights and dignity; not any kind of work but *meaningful* work.

- Agreed with Barth in prioritizing human work below the Sabbath rest.

---

32. Moltmann, *On Human Dignity*, 56–57.
33. Moltmann, *Theology of Play*, 64–65.

- Disagreed with Barth that work is simply to support our physical life—work has the joy of *existence* value.

- Believed that work does not define humans; we are loved by God first and created in God's image.

- Believed that work allows for human creativity and expression.

- Linked human work to Christ's suffering and resurrection.

- Supported working in community (as did Luther, Calvin, and Barth) and denounced unemployment as depriving humans of community.

- Looked forward (eschatologically) to the new creation with workers focused on the kingdom of God.

Miroslav Volf (born 1956)— Work in the Spirit

The purpose of a theology of work is to interpret, evaluate, and facilitate the transformation of human work. It can fulfill this purpose only if it takes the contemporary world of work seriously.[1]

MIROSLAV VOLF IS A Croatian Protestant theologian who studied under Moltmann, and earned a PhD in theology from the University of Tübingen. He is currently the Henry B. Wright Professor of Theology and Director of the Yale Center for Faith and Culture at Yale University. As a student of Moltmann, Volf is fully familiar with his eschatological theology of hope. He tries to integrate theology into today's work culture, economics, politics, and social realities to construct a theology of work. He wrote *Work in the Spirit: Toward a Theology of Work* after completing his dissertation on the same subject.

Volf sees our current society as becoming compartmentalized and individualistic, placing the Christian life in one segment and our work life in another segment. He believes that this trend is not true to the Christian faith. Christianity is a 24/7 faith and includes the workplace.[2] Modern work is driven more by self-realization than the theologically based Protestant work ethic. Human identity is defined through work accomplishments, which compels people to work harder. God has little to do with work. People worship themselves through their work. "Jobs seem to contribute

1. Volf, *Work in the Spirit*, 7.
2. Volf, *Work in the Spirit*, 13–14.

to major segments of people's identities—they influence awareness of who they are, where they have been, and where they can expect to go."[3]

More to Work Than Survival

He agrees with Barth on the need to work for survival, but follows Moltmann's and Cosden's belief that work must offer more than survival. If human beings simply follow Paul's injunction in 1 Thessalonians 4:12b and Ephesians 4:28 to work honestly to provide for "one's needs and the needs of one's community (especially its underprivileged members),"[4] then there is no need to develop a theology of work. Like Moltmann, Volf ties human work to the new creation: "When one refuses to assign eschatological significance to human work and makes it fully subservient to the vertical relation to God, one devalues human work and Christian cultural involvement."[5] His theology is also a theology of hope.

Three Normative Principles

Volf advocates that economic systems should have three normative principles. They are derived from the new creation based on Moltmann's eschatological theology. The first principle is *"guarding the individual's dignity."* Humans are created in the image of God which relates to self-actualization. The second principle is *"practicing solidarity."* This relates to community in which every person is a member. The third principle "implies the *responsibility of preserving the integrity of nature. Nature is not a mere thing."* This looks forward to the new creation.[6]

Unification of Work and Spiritual Life

A key concept of Volf's theology is that work and the spiritual life must be unified, or else human work has little meaning:

> Where the *vita activa* is fully subservient to the *vita contemplativa*, there is no need to reflect extensively on human work, since, as a

3. Volf, *Work in the Spirit*, 129–30.

4. Volf, *Work in the Spirit*, 149

5. Volf, *Work in the Spirit*, 90.

6. Volf, *Work in the Spirit*, 15–16 (emphasis his).

mere means to a much higher end, it is in the long run accidental to the real purpose of human life . . . I do propose, however, that *we treat them as two basic, alternating aspects of the Christian life that may differ in importance but that cannot be reduced one to another, and that form an inseparable unity.*[7]

Pneumatological Theology of Work

The main purpose of Volf's book "is to *develop a new—pneumatological* [doctrine of the Holy Spirit]—*theology* of work."[8] Like both Moltmann and Cosden, Volf seeks to integrate both Genesis and the New Testament into his theology of work.[9] Christian faith must be defined eschatologically or there is no faith. There is no separation between spiritual and secular life. As Volf notes, "Christian work must, therefore, be done under the inspiration of the Spirit and in the light of the coming new creation."[10] Our desires must be compatible for what God desires for God's creatures. Volf further adds, "And God desires the *new creation* for them."[11] Volf believes that only including the instrumental (self-realization) and relational (communal) aspects results in an inadequate theology of work model.[12]

Barth centered his work theology on the doctrine of creation (Genesis), and Moltmann's work theology points eschatologically to the new creation. Volf's theology is an open system (allows for change over time) that connects the doctrines of creation and new creation together through the eternal Spirit. As Volf wrote, "Through the Spirit, God is already working in history, using human actions to create provisional states of affairs that anticipate the new creation in a real way."[13] The doctrine of creation complements the doctrine of the new creation. The first creation must be preserved for God to transform it eschatologically into the new creation.[14] If only the doctrine of creation is used in a theology of work, then it will "justify the *status quo* and hinder needed change in both microeconomic

7. Volf, *Work in the Spirit*, 70 (emphasis his).
8. Volf, *Work in the Spirit*, 76 (emphasis his).
9. Volf, *Work in the Spirit*, 77.
10. Volf, *Work in the Spirit*, 79.
11. Volf, *Work in the Spirit*, 81 (emphasis his).
12. Volf, *Work in the Spirit*, 85.
13. Volf, *Work in the Spirit*, 100.
14. Volf, *Work in the Spirit*, 101.

and macroeconomic structures by appealing to divine preservation of the world."[15] Therefore, the Spirit of the new creation must be incorporated into a theology of work:

> Because the whole creation is the Spirit's sphere of operation, the Spirit is not only the Spirit of religious experience but also the Spirit of worldly engagement. For this reason it is not at all strange to connect the Spirit of God with mundane work.[16]

Volf uses Calvin's theology to support his beliefs in the spiritual aspects of work: "On the basis of passages like Exodus 31:2f, Calvin stressed that all human skills stem from the operation of the Spirit of God."[17]

How does one know how to use one's Spiritual gifts at work? Volf's answer is that, "The fruit of the Spirit [Gal. 5:22f.], which consists in the values of the new creation, determines how the gifts of the Spirit should be used."[18]

Sabbath

Volf does not advocate the Sabbath as strongly as Barth or Moltmann. He stresses a balance between work and leisure. Many contemporary workers find so much fulfillment in their work that it becomes their identity. Frenzied work is replaced by frenzied play. "Rest has been driven out of leisure,"[19] Volf says. Work and leisure should be balanced. Both should be present and work should make leisure possible. "If people are overworked," Volf says, "it is for the most part because they have a wrong attitude either to work or to their desires, not because they cannot otherwise meet their basic needs."[20] Although Volf acknowledges the Sabbath commandment, he does not place rest above work, as Barth did, or place the Sabbath on par with work, as did Moltmann and Cosden. Volf sees the Spirit as a 24/7 experience that should not be restricted.[21]

---

15. Volf, *Work in the Spirit*, 102 (emphasis his).

16. Volf, *Work in the Spirit*, 104.

17. Volf, *Work in the Spirit*, 130.

18. Volf, *Work in the Spirit*, 131.

19. Volf, *Work in the Spirit*, 135.

20. Volf, *Work in the Spirit*, 139–40.

21. Volf, *Work in the Spirit*, 141.

Vocation

Volf agrees with Luther's groundbreaking theology that all occupations, both active and contemplative, are of equal value: "Luther's notion of vocation *overcame the medieval hierarchy between* vita activa *and* vita contemplativa. Since every vocation rests on God's commission, every vocation is fundamentally of the same value before God."[22]

However, he rejects Luther's theology that God calls people to a certain station for life. Volf believes that vocation, as Luther defined it, "is not applicable to the increasingly mobile industrial and information society. Most people in these societies do not keep a single job or employment for a lifetime, but often switch from one job to another in the course of their active life." [23] Vocation has changed to gainful employment subject to market forces and a transformative society. "The reduction of vocation to employment," says Volf, "coupled with the belief that vocation is the primary service ordinary people render to God, contributed to the modern fateful elevation of work to the status of religion."[24]

Volf's pneumatological theology allows for the Spirit to send workers into different professions that take humanity toward the new creation. As Volf once wrote, "The charismatic nature of all Christian activity is the *theological* basis for a pneumatological understanding of work."[25] His break from Luther's vocational theology gives flexibility in employment options and occupations over time.[26]

Volf's reorientation of Luther's vocational theology into a pneumatological theology of work allows for an individual's gifts to be taken seriously. As Volf says, these gifts transform "work into a charismatic cooperation with God on the 'project' of the new creation."[27] If job changes align with the divine gift, then the worker is being faithful to God. Workers should be open to the Spirit and not worry about the absence of a permanent calling.[28] Luther understood vocational work as God calling humans to work, and Christians should answer God's call in obedience. In

22. Volf, *Work in the Spirit*, 106 (emphasis his).
23. Volf, *Work in the Spirit*, 108.
24. Volf, *Work in the Spirit*, 109.
25. Volf, *Work in the Spirit*, 113 (emphasis his).
26. Volf, *Work in the Spirit*, 116.
27. Volf, *Work in the Spirit*, 116.
28. Volf, *Work in the Spirit*, 116–17.

Volf's pneumatological theology of work, God "empowers and gifts them for work . . . They work, not primarily because it is their duty to work, but because they experience the inspiration and enabling of God's Spirit." Workers respond in "joyful willingness . . . Though not fully absent, the sense of duty gives way to the sense of inspiration."[29] While Luther believed that "one individual is *either* called to ministry *or* to secular work," Volf's Spirit theology of work is holistic: Christians can have various divine gifts that can be applied to both the sacred and secular.[30]

Dr. R. Paul Stevens, former David J. Brown Family Professor of Marketplace Theology and Leadership at Regent College (Vancouver, BC), challenges Volf's views on Luther's vocational theology. Stevens believes that placing spiritual work into both salvational and occupational work blurs the lines and, in a more secular society, salvational work becomes secondary. He writes:

> The problem with Volf's thesis, however, is not substantially different from that which Luther faced. When one secularizes spiritual gifts into all possible human occupations the line between gospel work and creation work will be blurred once again. More than likely, gospel work will be subsumed and secularized. Further, it is questionable whether there is any significant biblical evidence that Spirit-gifts are given for societal good rather than for building up the body of Christ.[31]

Dr. Stevens echoes Barth's comments. I understand the tightrope that Volf is theologically walking, but I side with Volf's thesis based on my professional work experience. My Christianity does not stop at the office door, and my spiritual gifts don't either.

Volf builds an excellent case for the spiritual aspect of the theology of work that balances the instrumental (self-actualization) and relational (communal) components. I believe it would have helped Volf's theological structure if he had created a clear threefold theological model, but we will leave that for the next part of this book. Volf does offer a limited Trinitarian statement.[32]

One of Volf's best qualities is that his writings are more in touch with current cultural realities. He uses clear language to describe complex

---

29. Volf, *Work in the Spirit*, 125.
30. Volf, *Work in the Spirit*, 156 (emphasis his).
31. Stevens, *Other Six Days*, 122.
32. Volf, *Work in the Spirit*, 133.

theological topics; for example: "All work that contradicts the new creation is meaningless; all work that corresponds to the new creation is ultimately meaningful."[33]

From the Reformation onward, I have presented exclusively Protestant theologians. However, the Catholic Church, starting in the nineteenth century, has also been at the forefront of developing a theology of work. In particular, a Polish pope who lived under communist rule has taken a leadership position.

In summary, Volf:

- Views our current society as becoming compartmentalized and individualistic, but Christianity is a 24/7 faith!

- Agrees with Moltmann that work is more than an activity to survive (breaks with Barth).

- Advocates three normative principles:

  1. Guarding the individual's dignity (self-actualization).

  2. Practicing solidarity (community).

  3. Preserving the integrity of nature (new creation).

- Unifies work and the spiritual life.

- Develops a pneumatological (Holy Spirit) theology of work (following Calvin, not Barth).

- Fuses the doctrine of creation (Genesis) and eschatology (new creation) together through the Holy Spirit.

- Stresses the balance between work and the Sabbath (following Moltmann, not Barth).

- Agrees with aspects of Luther's theology that all vocations are of equal value, but rejects Luther's premise that God calls people to a certain station. The Holy Spirit moves workers at different times to different stations.

33. Volf, *Work in the Spirit*, 121.

Pope John Paul II (1920–2005)— *Laborem exercens*

In the first place work is "for man" and not man "for work."[1]

ON MAY 15, 1891, Pope Leo XIII (1810–1903) published the encyclical *Rerum novarum* ("of revolutionary change"). Gregory Baum, former Canadian Catholic professor of theological ethics at McGill University, called this the starting point for what is usually known as "papal social teaching."[2] On September 14, 1981, ninety years after *Rerum novarum*, Pope John Paul II, born Karol Józef Wojtyla in communist Poland and canonized in 2014, published the encyclical *Laborem exercens* ("Through Work"), which furthered the Catholic Church's social teachings and developed its theology of work. The encyclical began with a general definition of work:

> Work means any activity by man, whether manual or intellectual, whatever its nature or circumstances; it means any human activity that can and must be recognized as work, in the midst of all the many activities of which man is capable and to which he is predisposed by his very nature, by virtue of humanity itself.[3]

1. Baum, *Priority of Labor*, 106.
2. Baum, *Priority of Labor*, 5.
3. Baum, *Priority of Labor*, 95.

Volf's Criticism of Pope John Paul's Definition of Work

Volf finds the Catholic definition of work in Pope John Paul's encyclical *Laborem exercens* to be too general and "odd." He advocates a definition that separates work from other activities, rather than "any activity by man." Volf summarizes his concerns by stating: "So work is finally whatever one thinks work is."[4]

Like Moltmann, Volf is concerned about human dignity and "oppressive misuse"[5] of workers. He proposes another definition of work that includes community and self-expression:

> Work is honest, purposeful, and methodologically specified social activity whose primary goal is the creation of products or states of affairs that can satisfy the needs of working individuals or their co-creatures, or (if primarily an end in itself) activity that is necessary in order for acting individuals to satisfy their needs apart from the need for the activity itself.[6]

> What distinguishes pleasant work from a useful hobby is that work must be either necessary to satisfy needs other than the worker's need for the activity itself or be not primarily done for its own sake.[7]

Catholic Theology of Work

Pope John Paul II used both Genesis and Christ as the two primary scriptural sources for his theology of work. In Genesis, only humans worked, and they worked within community. Humans from the very beginning were called by God to work. Work differentiates humans from other creatures as only humans work. For man, work occupies "his existence on earth" operating within human community. "And this mark decides its interior characteristics; in a sense it constitutes its very nature."[8] Pope John Paul II quotes Genesis 1:27–28 to support God's desire for humans to work, "even

---

4. Volf, *Work in the Spirit*, 7.
5. Volf, *Work in the Spirit*, 9.
6. Volf, *Work in the Spirit*, 10–11.
7. Volf, *Work in the Spirit*, 12.
8. Baum, *Priority of Labor*, 95.

though these words do not refer directly and explicitly to work." He states that these verses are "its very deepest essence." This mandate is to dominate the earth. He says, "In carrying out this mandate, man, every human being, reflects the very action of the Creator of the universe."[9]

Like Moltmann and Cosden, Pope John Paul II's view of work is more than instrumental, it is also self-actualization. Because humans are made in the image of God, they have the ability to make rational decisions "with a tendency to self-realization. As a person, man is therefore the subject of work."[10]

Work is Part of Being Human and Transformational

Pope John Paul II also agreed with Cosden that work is part of being human and transformational. Pope John Paul II states the positive benefits of work. Not only is work good for humanity and nature, but it also helps humans achieve fulfillment.[11] He quotes doctrine from the Second Vatican Council about work being integral to self-actualization:

> For when a man works, he not only alters things and society, he develops himself as well. He learns much, he cultivates his resources, he goes outside of himself and beyond himself. Rightly understood, this kind of growth is of greater value than any external riches which can be garnered.[12]

Pope John Paul II used the working life of Jesus Christ as support for the value of human work. Jesus worked as a craftsman. The one who proclaimed the gospel modeled "the gospel of work." While Jesus did not state any direct commandments to work and he did direct humans to not worry about work and life, his life alone was "unequivocal" proof that, "He belongs to the 'working world,' he has appreciation and respect for human work."[13]

---

9. Baum, *Priority of Labor*, 101.

10. Baum, *Priority of Labor*, 104–5.

11. Baum, *Priority of Labor*, 112.

12. Baum, *Priority of Labor*, 146.

13. Baum, *Priority of Labor*, 144–45.

Work is a Fundamental Human Right

Like Moltmann, Pope John Paul II viewed work as a fundamental human right. "The human rights that flow from work are part of the broader context of those fundamental rights of the person."[14] He takes the macro view that Christianity changed the perception of work when God became human, as Jesus, and did manual work. The value of work is not the work, but the worker. "The sources of the dignity of work are to be sought primarily in the subjective dimension, not in the objective one."[15] Pope John Paul II focuses work on the person, not the outcome or product.

Unemployment is an "Evil"

He called unemployment an "evil" which had social implications and paralleled Moltmann's theology that full employment was a human right—the lack of work can "become a real social disaster."[16] Pope John Paul II places the burden of addressing unemployment on governmental organizations that should rectify unemployment through laws and education.

All of this leads Pope John Paul II to state his central theology of work:

> The primary basis of the value of work is man himself, who is its subject. This leads immediately to a very important conclusion of an ethical nature: However true it may be that man is destined for work and called to it, in the first place work is "for man" and not man "for work" [my emphasis] . . . Man is treated as an instrument of production, whereas he—he alone, independent of the work he does—ought to be treated as the effective subject of work and its true maker and creator.[17]

While Pope John Paul II was not against capital, he ranked capital below human work. Capital is just "a collection of things," but "man alone is a person."[18] Church teachings have always prioritized human labor over capital.[19] While other theologians have hinted at the importance of the worker, Pope John Paul II articulates this fact best.

14. Baum, *Priority of Labor*, 126.

15. Baum, *Priority of Labor*, 105–6.

16. Baum, *Priority of Labor*, 129–30.

17. Baum, *Priority of Labor*, 106–7.

18. Baum, *Priority of Labor*, 119.

19. Baum, *Priority of Labor*, 117.

Sabbath

The Sabbath had its place in Pope John Paul II's theology of work, but it was not as high as Barth's placement of it. Just as workers should imitate God in their work, humans should imitate God in rest. Since God rested on the seventh day, humans should also rest from their labors. Not only is rest required on the Sabbath, but it is also a time for "man to prepare himself, by becoming more and more what in the will of God he ought to be."[20] So the Sabbath is a time of preparation and seeking guidance from God.

Work of the Spirit

The work of the Spirit and the new creation was mentioned at the end of the encyclical. The Spirit is at work: "He animates, purifies and strengthens those noble longings too by which the human family strives to make its life more human and to render the whole earth submissive to this goal." Pope John Paul II warns his flock to carefully distinguish human progress from the new creation. However, if human progress "can contribute to the better ordering of human society, it is of vital concern to the kingdom of God."[21] Pope John Paul II seemed to be more focused on stressing the priority of humans over their labors than in humans laboring with the spirit toward the new creation.

Laborem exercens went into more detail about modern work than any other theology of work discussed so far. The encyclical discussed wages and social benefits, supported the rights of unions, upheld the dignity of agricultural work ("the world of agriculture, which provides society with the goods it needs for its daily sustenance, is of fundamental importance"[22]), supported the rights of disabled persons to work, and placed boundaries on immigration.

20. Baum, *Priority of Labor*, 143.
21. Baum, *Priority of Labor*, 148.
22. Baum, *Priority of Labor*, 137.

Community

Throughout the encyclical, Pope John Paul II emphasized community. Work unites people. Work has the power to build community. Workers, managers of work, and owners of capital must all unite in community.[23]

Pope John Paul II and the Catholic Church focused on the issues of the poor and liberation theologies ("various 20th-century theological movements which see the gospel as liberation from all forms of oppression—economic, spiritual, political, and social"[24]). He was concerned about the unemployed, marginalized, handicapped, poor, and all those who carried the burden of toil and labor under oppressive conditions. While Pope John Paul II's theology of work emphasizes different elements than other modern Protestant theologians, he was more aligned than not. As Timothy Keller writes:

> Many have pointed out the similarities between the Catholic understanding of natural law and the Reformed understanding of common grace, namely, that God gives wisdom and insight to all people, including non-Christians, so they can enrich the world through their work. In summary, today there is no longer a great divide between Catholic social teaching on the importance of work and that of the Protestant Reformation.[25]

In a world where so many humans toil under oppressive conditions to barely have enough food to eat, *Laborem exercens* is refreshing to read. Humans are more important than material things. Economics as a science treats human labor as instruments of production. This is why work and faith are so important. Christians in the workplace must prioritize humans over material things in order to be obedient to God.

In summary, Pope John Paul II:

- Used both Genesis and the life of Christ to support his theology of work.

- Agreed with Cosden that work is part of being human and is transformational.

- Agreed with Moltmann that work is a fundamental human right.

23. Baum, *Priority of Labor*, 135–36.

24. McKim, *Westminster Dictionary of Theological Terms*, 160.

25. Keller, *Every Good Endeavor*, 268–69.

- Called unemployment "evil," which parallels Moltmann's belief that full employment was a human right.

- Stated that the value of work is man himself, who is the subject: *work is for man and not man for work.*

- Placed the Sabbath and work on relatively equal footing, similar to both Moltmann and Volf.

- Ranked human work above material "things" like capital and land.

- Agreed with Volf and others that a necessary component of work is self-actualization.

- Emphasized both the work of the Holy Spirit and community.

Based on my research, which is summarized in part I, the foundations are now in place to build a practical theological model on work for Christians in the workplace. This is developed in part II.

PART II

A Theological Model of Work

In Part I, we reviewed the Scripture references and the history of Christian theological writings on work. We have seen how the early Christians did not separate their spiritual lives from their active work lives. During medieval times, after the church and state were combined, spiritual life was superior to work life. Those who worked in church vocations were viewed as more pleasing to God than those in all other vocations. The Protestant Reformers used Scripture (1 Pet 2:9) to strike down this hierarchical separation and expose corruption in the church. The Protestant work ethic ushered in profound industrial growth and scholastic enlightenment. Human reasoning started to shape society.

By the nineteenth century, Western Christians believed that, with education and reasoning, humans could solve the problems of the world. Then the world experienced two devastating wars during the twentieth century. Theologians such as Barth pushed back on human reasoning and advocated returning to God's revelation through Scripture: We know God best through Jesus Christ. Work is important to sustain life, but humans were created to rest in God. In recent times, theologians have focused on human self-actualization, the Holy Spirit, and striving toward the new creation.

How do we look back on 2,000 years of Christian work theology and then apply it? We start with a simple model that is both theologically and practically supported. Second, we make sure that the model is easily understandable and can be depicted in a simple diagram. And third, it must be easily applied in our daily work lives. Working Christians in all occupations should be able to use this model.

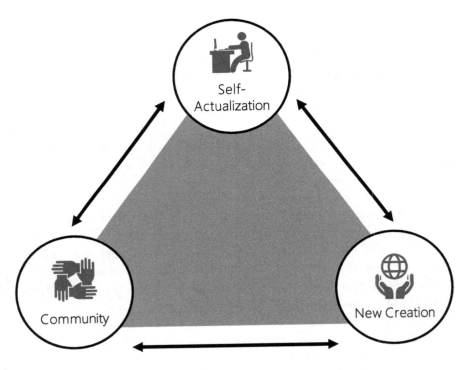

Figure 8—Proposed Theological Model of Work

Theological Model

The Christian life is essentially unbalanced and fragmented when God intends it to be unified. A better way involves viewing the human vocation in terms of a covenant encompassing creation, redemption and final consummation. Salvation is both a rescue operation (recovering our lost vocation in Eden) and a completion project (preparing for the final renewal of creation at the second coming of Jesus). Eschatology (the end times) is critical to understanding our vocation as Christians in this world.[1]

—R. PAUL STEVENS, PROFESSOR OF MARKETPLACE THEOLOGY

MY PROPOSED THEOLOGICAL MODEL is founded on the threefold, distinct, and interrelating aspects of Christian work: self-actualization, community, and new creation. All three aspects must be present in our work; no aspect has priority over the others. Just as a three-legged stool must have all legs balanced to function properly, so must this theological model of work. The model is Trinitarian, as each work aspect relates to a person of the Trinity. It is a distinct, nonhierarchical, and interrelational representation:

Miroslav Volf, a contemporary theologian highlighted in part I, indirectly alludes to this model in his book, *Work in the Spirit*. He states that his own development is critical to the new creation. But one lives in community so that must also be a part of the new creation. Individual development must benefit others. "My development must be attuned to the well-being of the whole creation." Work must integrate and unite "individuals, society, and nature."[2]

1. Stevens, *Other Six Days*, 89–90.
2. Volf, *Work in the Spirit*, 131–32.

Self-actualization is focused on the individual—what God created within humans in God's image. God created humans to be relational within community based on the life and teachings of Jesus Christ. New creation is focused on following the Holy Spirit in establishing God's kingdom here on earth. Ken Costa, former British Chairman of Lazard and Chairman of Alpha International, emphasizes this truth: "God had the desire to create for us on earth the same attributes of sharing, service, partnership and collaboration that are enjoyed in the Godhead."[3]

Theological Professor Darrell Cosden's threefold theological aspects of work, as detailed in his book *A Theology of Work*, are:

- Instrumental—"a means to continued survival,"

- Relational—"human existential realization and fulfillment,"[4] and

- Ontological—"a fundamental facet of our human and created existence."[5]

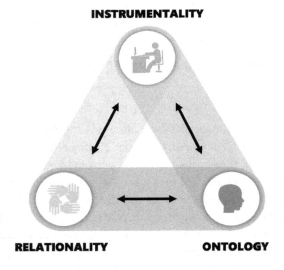

INSTRUMENTALITY

RELATIONALITY   **ONTOLOGY**

Figure 9—Cosden's Theological Model of Work (Author's Visual Representation)

While I liked Cosden's model, the three aspects did not clearly separate certain attributes. For example, in the instrumentality dimension,

3. Costa, *God at Work*, 18.
4. Cosden, *Theology of Work*, 11–12.
5. Cosden, *Theology of Work*, 177.

Cosden includes utility (providing substance), community (needs of other fellow creatures) and spirituality (character development, sanctification). I propose an alternative theological model that rearranges the attributes into three clearer distinctions corresponding to the Trinity.

Self-Actualization

Work is as much a basic human need as food, beauty, rest, friendship, prayer, and sexuality; it is not simply medicine but food for our soul. Without meaningful work we sense significant inner loss and emptiness.[1]

—TIMOTHY KELLER, FORMER SENIOR PASTOR
OF REDEEMER PRESBYTERIAN CHURCH

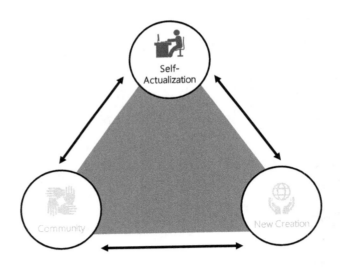

Figure 10—Self-Actualization Aspect of Work

HUMANS ARE CREATED IN the image of God, as stated in Genesis 1:

> Then God said, "Let us make humankind in our image, according to our likeness; and let them have dominion over the fish of the

1. Keller, *Every Good Endeavor*, 23.

sea, and over the birds of the air, and over the cattle, and over all the wild animals of the earth, and over every creeping thing that creeps upon the earth."

So God created humankind in his image, in the image of God he created them; male and female he created them.

God blessed them, and God said to them, "Be fruitful and multiply, and fill the earth and subdue it; and have dominion over the fish of the sea and over the birds of the air and over every living thing that moves upon the earth." God said, "See, I have given you every plant yielding seed that is upon the face of all the earth, and every tree with seed in its fruit; you shall have them for food. And to every beast of the earth, and to every bird of the air, and to everything that creeps on the earth, everything that has the breath of life, I have given every green plant for food." And it was so. God saw everything that he had made, and indeed, it was very good. And there was evening and there was morning, the sixth day. (Gen 1:26–31)

Jürgen Moltmann gives an excellent summary of what it means for humankind to be made in the image of God. Of all the creatures created by God, humans alone were created in the image of God, who finds "his partner, his echo, and his honor." Being made in God's image, humans are God's representatives on earth and exhibit God's goodness. Humans therefore occupy a special position, "an image of what he loves and fears."[2] "As God's image, men and women are his counterpart in the work of creation. The human being is the Other who resembles God (Ps. 8.5)."[3]

Before our modern age, with its emphasis on education, work primarily concentrated on meeting human physiological needs. All theologians agree that humans must work to survive, and God's providence sustains humankind. For many humans today, working to meet human physiological needs is their only focus, as this consumes the majority of their time and energy. For example, millions of women walk miles just to get water. Survival depends on it, and other human needs are secondary. As we reviewed in part I, modern theologians have recognized that God created humankind to thrive beyond physiological needs. In 1943, *Psychological Review* published a groundbreaking article by Abraham Maslow (1908–1970) titled "A Theory of Human Motivation."[4] In this secular article, Maslow

2. Moltmann, *On Human Being*, 108–9.

3. Moltmann, *God in Creation*, 77–78.

4. Maslow, "Theory of Human Motivation," 370–96.

outlined the hierarchy of human needs: physiological, safety, love/belonging, esteem, and self-actualization.

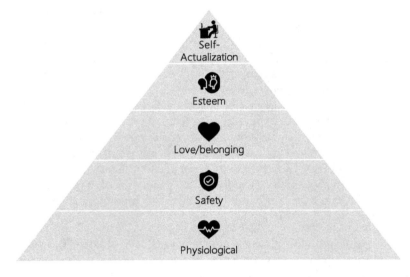

Figure 11—Maslow's Hierarchy of Human Needs

These human needs were created by God, and humankind has been climbing this hierarchal ladder since creation. God gave humans gifts, diverse in both degree and type, and these gifts are a reflection or image of God. But for humankind to be fully human, our work should strive toward self-actualization.

It is important to understand Maslow's theory. Human needs, from the most primary (physiological) to the highest (self-actualization), depend on each other, with the lowest tier requiring satisfaction before the highest can be realized: "the appearance of one need usually rests on the prior satisfaction of another."[5]

The first and most basic need is physiological—the human survival requirement for food and water. Humans cannot survive for very long without meeting this most basic need. All theologians agree on this. Dr. Cosden states that the theology of work is not meaningful "without paying particular attention to issues relating to sustenance."[6]

5. Maslow, *Theory of Human Motivation*, 1.
6. Cosden, *Theology of Work*, 181.

Maslow described the physiological needs, such as food, as human's most basic need. Humans that are "extremely and dangerously hungry" will have no other interest except for seeking food.[7] For many people who live in poverty, physiological needs dominate, as hunger is a constant threat to their survival. God did not create humans to *only* do their work for food. When food is plentiful and the physiological need is filled, then other needs emerge. "A want that is satisfied is no longer a want." [8]

In our earlier review of Karl Barth's work theology, we saw that he places criteria for work around activities to prolong human life, "to earn their daily bread and a little more."[9] Based on Maslow's theory of human motivation, I disagree with Barth, as God created human work to be more than simply foraging for food to prolong life. Barth realized self-actualization (his ground-breaking theological work) because he had not only his physical needs satisfied, but all the other lower human needs.

If humans are physiologically satisfied with food and water, they look next for protection. In the modern world, safety is achieved through government defense funding, savings accounts, insurance coverage, and even religion.[10] Karl Barth was able to achieve self-actualization because he was a tenured professor. When he stood up to the Nazi government by writing the *Barman Declaration* (1934) and lost his University of Bonn academic position in 1935, he needed safety and found it in Switzerland at the University of Basel. Had Barth remained in Germany, it is highly likely that he would have died during the war and not published his *Church Dogmatics*. He sought safety, and for good reason: It allowed him to reach self-actualization. All humans need safety before self-actualization can be achieved.

After physiological and safety needs are achieved, Maslow believed, the third human motivation level is the need for "love and affection and belongingness." Humans are social animals and need to feel love, whether from friends, family, spouse, or lover. People will hunger for affection and inclusiveness within a group. Once physiological and safety needs are satisfied, humans desire community, where love is given and received.[11] Humans are not made to be alone. God created this human need in the image of the Trinity relationship and said, "Be fruitful and multiply" (Gen 1:28).

7. Maslow, *Theory of Human Motivation*, 2–3.

8. Maslow, *Theory of Human Motivation*, 4.

9. Barth, *Doctrine of Creation*, 3:525.

10. Maslow, *Theory of Human Motivation*, 4–6.

11. Maslow, *Theory of Human Motivation*, 6–7.

Franciscan Friar Richard Rohr writes "that human personhood is a *subsistent relation* at its core, generating, in fact, relationships of unconditional love with the same standing as the persons of the Trinity." [12] When we work and live without love or relationships, we lack the ability to self-actualize since our need to give and receive love comes before self-actualization. We are human through giving and receiving love.

Maslow's fourth level of hierarchical human needs is self-esteem. People desire self-respect and to be respected by other people. Self-esteem is divided into two components. The first is "the desire for strength, for achievement, for adequacy, for confidence in the face of the world, and for independence and freedom." The second is the desire to be appreciated by other people.[13] The human need for self-esteem is difficult for some Christians to accept, as Christ says, "I am gentle and humble in heart" (Matt 11:29). Paul repetitively states that Christians are to exhibit humility and meekness: "As God's chosen ones, holy and beloved, clothe yourselves with compassion, kindness, humility, meekness, and patience" (Col 3:12). But self-esteem is an inner, individual need and should not be confused with boasting or egotism. Jesus taught us to "love your neighbor as yourself" (Matt 19:19), but if one doesn't love the self first, then one cannot love the neighbor. The self-respect component of self-esteem brings forth self-confidence. We know from studies that children grow self-confident when they're encouraged and praised. Children who receive constant negativity have less self-confidence and, on average, achieve less.

Athletes strive to win, not just because it improves the physical body, but because it brings self-esteem. When I ran marathons, I raced against the clock and my standing within my age group. Running improved my self-esteem, especially when my race times or age group placement improved. This, in turn, drove me to train harder and more effectively. However, at the end of the race, I congratulated my fellow competitors who pushed me to perform at a higher level, and I gained strong friendships through competition. I did not boast of my achievements nor downgrade my competitors, but my self-esteem increased when I did well and achieved my goals.

Possessing self-esteem, humans can then strive toward the highest human motivation need of self-actualization (in part I, the term *self-realization* was used by several theologians). When all the other needs are satisfied, humans still desire what they are "fitted for . . . What a man *can* be,

12. Rohr and Morrell, *Divine Dance*, 74.
13. Maslow, *Theory of Human Motivation*, 7.

he *must* be." Self-actualization is actually being what one has the potential to be. "This tendency might be phrased as the desire to become more and more what one is, to become everything that one is capable of becoming."[14] Dr. Darrell Cosden theologically follows Maslow. He argues that a theology of work "must allow room for human self-expression, self-exploration and personal development in and through human working activity." Humans are "open beings" and on a journey of discovering their being. Work, while not the only part of the journey of life, is "a central contributor to the evolution of the self both individually and socially."[15] Self-actualization is fundamental (existential) to humans, and our work can lead to self-actualization provided our lower needs are met. Maslow wrote, "We shall call people who are satisfied in these needs, basically satisfied people, and it is from these that we may expect the fullest (and healthiest) creativeness."[16]

While the five human motivation needs are hierarchical, each need does not have to be fully satisfied before advancing to the higher needs. It is normal that lower needs may not be fully satisfied before higher needs are partially satisfied. The percentage of fulfillment does decrease as one goes up from the lower to higher needs.[17] It is important to note that self-actualization cannot be achieved within societies that do not have basic human rights. "Such conditions as freedom to speak, freedom to do what one wishes so long as no harm is done to others, freedom to express one's self, freedom to investigate and seek for information, freedom to defend one's self, justice, fairness, honesty, orderliness in the group are examples of such preconditions for basic need satisfactions."[18]

Self-actualization is focused on the individual. It is meant to be individualistic and may make some Christians uncomfortable since it is so self-oriented. However, if Christians focus *only* on self-actualization without the balance of the other two aspects of community and new creation, then the work theology model fails. All three aspects must be fulfilled and balanced for the model to be satisfied. This leads to the next aspect: community.

---

14. Maslow, *Theory of Human Motivation*, 7–8 (emphasis his).
15. Cosden, *Theology of Work*, 183.
16. Maslow, *Theory of Human Motivation*, 8.
17. Maslow, *Theory of Human Motivation*, 11.
18. Maslow, *Theory of Human Motivation*, 8.

Community

Jesus' life and the way he acted was related to community, and it was therefore always a receiving and an acting on behalf of other people, and in their stead.[1]

—DR. JÜRGEN MOLTMANN

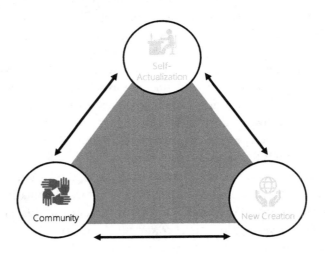

Figure 12—Community Aspect of Work

PRACTICALLY ALL WRITINGS REGARDING work and faith state how important community is to human work and how central it is to Christianity. Community is fundamental to many other religions, as well as the non-religious. If you ask people what community means, you will hear a wide range of definitions: family, friends, geography, culture, religion, language, gender, age, sport, etc. If you ask whether community is a positive or

1. Moltmann, *Way of Jesus Christ*, 147.

negative experience, you'll find that most view it positively, unless a community harms other persons or other communities. According to American Episcopal theologian Dr. Matthew Fox, the definition of community is "to work on a common task together." He believes that workers should ask themselves this question: "How can my work create good work for others?"[2]

Community differs from society, and Jürgen Moltmann describes the difference as "two opposed basic possibilities of human corporate life." Community is an original, permanent, and interwoven part of life while society is a transient, man-made institution. "Society is always a product of the falling apart of the original community."[3]

Humans are made for relationships and need community, as illustrated in Maslow's third need of love/belonging. Even more basic than love and belonging is physiological need, which is also tied to community. For example, the physiological needs of a child are supplied by parents or other caregivers for many years. Children would die shortly after birth unless someone takes care of them. Community is fundamental to humanity since, as English poet John Donne stated, "No man is an island." Community is also relational, which Richard Rohr eloquently describes: "Relationships are entwined, entrenched, elusive, messy, enabling, enrapturing, maddening, exhilarating, frustrating, exposing, and too beautiful for words."[4]

Community balances self-actualization. If we disregard community during the climb to self-actualization, then we may destroy other humans or their ability to obtain self-actualization. American author and commentator David Brooks wrote, "We have an innate tendency toward selfishness and overconfidence. We have a tendency to see ourselves as the center of the universe, as if everything revolves around us."[5] Ken Costa's view on community is that "God is interested in building up his original plan of community." The reason for work is not confined only to self-fulfillment, but also "in the context of the needs of the wider human community."[6]

While working in the corporate world for thirty-four years, I witnessed many instances of self-actualization undermining community. There were times when I thought other employees worked for different companies. Employees fought turf warfare. Bitter rivalries for individual power destroyed

---

2. Fox, *Reinvention of Work*, 135–36.

3. Moltmann, *On Human Being*, 61.

4. Rohr and Morrell, *Divine Dance*, 21.

5. Brooks, *Road to Character*, 262.

6. Costa, *God at Work*, 30.

financial value. Managers transferred employees with performance issues and poor behaviors to unknowing managers rather than doing the difficult work of mentoring those employees. Luckily, these were the exceptions, as the majority of my fellow employees understood community and the need to work together for the greater good of society.

Reverend Timothy Keller writes:

> If the point of work is to serve and exalt ourselves, then our work inevitably becomes less about the work and more about us. Our aggressiveness will eventually become abuse, our drive will become burnout, and our self-sufficiency will become self-loathing. But if the purpose of work is to serve and exalt something *beyond* ourselves, then we actually have a better reason to deploy our talent, ambition, and entrepreneurial vigor—and we are more likely to be successful in the long run, even by the world's definition.[7]

We have all read about individuals and companies that knowingly destroy the environment for monetary gains. History provides a long list of governments that sought power and territory by invading other countries. Neighbors fight over silly issues rather than discussing their differences and deciding what is best for their community, not the individual. A person's self-actualization is shaped within community and individuals form community.

Jesus Christ came into the world for humankind's salvation but also to teach us about community. Early in Jesus' ministry, he formed a community of disciples to personally teach them about God's kingdom and how individuals should relate to one another within community. In the Gospel of Matthew (5:1—7:27), Jesus teaches about community in his Sermon on the Mount:

- You have heard that it was said to those of ancient times, "You shall not murder"; and "whoever murders shall be liable to judgment." But I say to you that if you are angry with a brother or sister, you will be liable to judgment; and if you insult a brother or sister, you will be liable to the council; and if you say, "You fool," you will be liable to the hell of fire (Matt 5:21).

- You have heard that it was said, "You shall love your neighbor and hate your enemy." But I say to you, Love your enemies and pray for those who persecute you (Matt 5:43–44).

---

7. Keller, *Every Good Endeavor*, 57–58 (emphasis his).

- Do not store up for yourselves treasures on earth, where moth and rust consume and where thieves break in and steal; but store up for yourselves treasures in heaven, where neither moth nor rust consumes and where thieves do not break in and steal. For where your treasure is, there your heart will be also (Matt 6:19–21).

- In everything do to others as you would have them do to you; for this is the law and the prophets (Matt 7:12).

Jesus was pointing his followers toward God's kingdom and introducing the new age. He was the fulfillment of the kingdom, although the world was not yet the kingdom. Was this theoretical or practical advice? Moltmann clearly believed that all of God's people are expected to follow Jesus' sermon: "community exists in the hearing of Jesus' word, and in the *doing* of it."[8]

Jesus taught in parables, many of which were about living in community:

- The Good Samaritan (Luke 10:29)—the treatment of our neighbor (love).

- The Prodigal Son (Luke 15:11)—the welcoming of the lost back into community (love and forgiveness).

- Two Debtors (Luke 7:36–50)—forgiving debts (love and forgiveness).

- Talents (Matt 25:14–30)—using your personal gifts (service).

Through the lens of Scripture, we better understand God, and the best way to understand God is through Jesus' teachings and life on earth.[9] Jesus taught community by example. During his last community meal, the Last Supper, Jesus served his disciples bread and said, "Take; this is my body," and then served the wine and said, "This is my blood of the covenant, which is poured out for many" (Mark 14:22–24). The next day, Jesus' words became action when he was crucified. The Last Supper is also called *Communion*, which is derived from the same Latin word as *community*. In many Christian churches, the Lord's Supper can be administered only in open or corporate Christian community since Jesus served the meal in community. The same applies to baptism, as it is a community event. A child or adult is publicly brought into the Christian community through

8. Moltmann, *Way of Jesus Christ*, 127.
9. Costa, *God at Work*, 41–42.

either communal acceptance to raise the child in the Christian faith or a self-pronouncement of Christian faith. These two essential Christian sacraments show how central community is to Christianity. Work outside of or disregarding community is not Christian. It goes directly against the life and teachings of Christ. John Wesley taught that "the Bible knows nothing of solitary religion."[10]

In part I, we explored the monastic movement's rise during the early Christian period. This solitary existence was eventually frowned upon because people could not serve their neighbors when isolated. As Dr. Stevens writes:

> *Good work is communal.* It is a means of building community and serving our neighbors. We are called to work *together*, in partnership. Work and its organizations impact social structures and the social order. We become who we are in relationship.[11]

This led to communal monasteries. Some served others only within the monastery, while others chose to be open to external, nonmonastic communities. This led to a hierarchical relationship between clergy and laypersons. Reformers fought against monastic communities because Scripture does not support divided communities, as all are united together in Christ.

Martin Luther divided his work theology into two kingdoms: the spiritual and the temporal. In the temporal world, our work is directed toward our neighbor, which is what Jesus taught and embodied during his ministry. Our neighbors are not just the Christians we know; they begin with our family and extend to communities far away from our homes. When we close off the world and withdraw, as did past monastic communities (and some still withdraw to a limited extent today), we move away from community and the teachings of Christ. Our work should be within community, not isolated from it. Christian community is a missional community, not a closed community. Obedience to Christ is being *active in* and *serving within* community. Building and enhancing community is fundamental to Christian work and forms one of the three aspects of the theology of work model. Without it, self-actualization goes unchecked, and we cannot take the journey toward the new creation.

10. Stevens, *Other Six Days*, 63.
11. Stevens, *Work Matters*, 19 (emphasis his).

New Creation

Christian faith is eschatological. Christian life is life in the Spirit
of the new creation or it is not Christian life at all.[1]

—DR. MIROSLAV VOLF

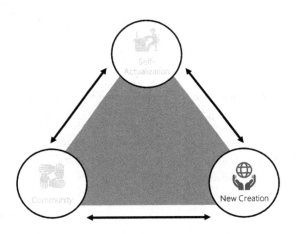

Figure 13—New Creation Aspect of Work

WITH COMMUNITY AS THE second aspect in our work theology, we next
look toward the new creation. As Moltmann wrote, "In the New Testament
the divine righteousness is accordingly understood by Paul as God's faithfulness in communal relationships, as an event brought about by God, and
as an event from which there arises a new creation and new life."[2] Without
community, there is no hope of human progression toward the new creation. Our role as Christians in the workplace is not to continually look

1. Volf, *Work in the Spirit*, 79.
2. Moltmann, *Theology of Hope*, 205.

back at history to solve earthly problems (yes, we can learn from history), but to look forward toward fulfilling the new creation.[3] Our work is meaningless when we work against the fulfillment of the new creation.[4] Miroslav Volf agrees with his teacher, Dr. Moltmann: "A theological interpretation of work is valid only if it facilitates transformation of work toward ever-greater correspondence with the coming new creation."[5]

The new creation is defined theologically as the anticipated renewal of the world by God. Some Scripture references discussing the new creation include:

- Then I saw a new heaven and a new earth; for the first heaven and the first earth had passed away, and the sea was no more (Rev 21:1).

- I consider that the sufferings of this present time are not worth comparing with the glory about to be revealed to us. For the creation waits with eager longing for the revealing of the children of God; for the creation was subjected to futility, not of its own will but by the will of the one who subjected it, in hope that the creation itself will be set free from its bondage to decay and will obtain the freedom of the glory of the children of God (Rom 8:18–21).

- But, in accordance with his promise, we wait for new heavens and a new earth, where righteousness is at home (2 Pet 3:13).

The new creation can also be defined as the new life brought to Christians by Jesus Christ through the power of the Holy Spirit. An example of this new creation definition is found in 2 Corinthians 5:17: "So if anyone is in Christ, there is a new creation."

While the preceding definition of new creation is important, it is not exactly the same as the kingdom. Scripture speaks about the kingdom in various ways:

- Kingdom: ". . . your kingdom is an everlasting kingdom" (Ps 145:13) and "Your kingdom come" (Matt 6:10).

- The kingdom of God: "How hard it will be for those who have wealth to enter the kingdom of God" (Mark 10:23)!

---

3. Moltmann, *Theology of Hope*, 298.

4. Volf, *Work in the Spirit*, 121.

5. Volf, *Work in the Spirit*, 83.

- The kingdom of Christ and of God: ". . . that no fornicator or impure person, or one who is greedy (that is, an idolater), has any inheritance in the kingdom of Christ and of God" (Eph 5:5).

- The kingdom of heaven: "Blessed are the poor in spirit, for theirs is the kingdom of heaven" (Matt 5:3).

- Kingdom of our Lord and Savior Jesus Christ: ". . . entry into the eternal kingdom of our Lord and Savior Jesus Christ will be richly provided for you" (2 Pet 1:11).

"Kingdom" is quoted in Scripture in various ways, but all relate to the kingdom of God. Dr. Armand Larive writes, "The kingdom of God should be one of the most important doctrines for working people because it is the shared venue for the work of God and the work of the people. It signifies the locus of God's reign and activity."[6]

The kingdom of God will be established in the new creation and has come in Jesus, whose "driving passion was to declare the coming of the kingdom, God's kingdom."[7] Luke 17:20–21 states:

> Once Jesus was asked by the Pharisees when the kingdom of God was coming, and he answered, "The kingdom of God is not coming with things that can be observed; nor will they say, 'Look, here it is!' or 'There it is!' For, in fact, the kingdom of God is among you."

For this book, I will follow Moltmann's format in defining all these kingdom terms as the new creation.[8]

The new creation is probably the least understood of the three aspects in the model of work, just as the Holy Spirit is probably the least understood person of the Trinity. Both point to the future rather than the past. Dr. Fox writes:

> Work is about the future. Therefore it is about fulfilling dreams, achieving promises, and entering into mysteries greater than ourselves and greater than our own work. This makes work eschatological. Good work is about hope. It brings hope and awakens others to hope.[9]

---

6. Larive, *After Sunday*, 56.

7. Stevens, *Work Matters*, 135.

8. Moltmann, *Way of Jesus Christ*, 98.

9. Fox, *Reinvention of Work*, 107.

Many Christians see the new creation as only the end of time. This is partially correct, but the Holy Spirit is also working through history toward the new creation.[10] Creation and Jesus are historic events, while the future is speculative. This is why the new creation is the most difficult aspect to comprehend. Christians today want to know the future, and Jesus' disciples were no different. Just prior to Christ's ascension, the disciples wanted to know when the kingdom would be restored:

> He [Jesus] replied, "It is not for you to know the times or periods that the Father has set by his own authority. But you will receive power when the Holy Spirit has come upon you; and you will be my witnesses in Jerusalem, in all Judea and Samaria, and to the ends of the earth." (Acts 1:7–8)

The Holy Spirit inspires persons to become and remain Christians. The Holy Spirit leads Christians toward the new creation. Obedience to God is obedience to the Holy Spirit in our work. One of our priorities at work should be taking steps toward the new creation. We "*become* real" when "the Spirit that made the heavens and the Earth can flow through us and effect its New Creation through us."[11] Our time on earth *does* concern God as we were created for self-actualization that builds community and draws humanity nearer to the new creation. Volf writes, "What people desire is objectively desirable only when it corresponds to what the loving and just God desires for them as God's creatures. And God desires the *new creation* for them."[12] David Jensen concurs: "What we do with the time we have *matters*. It matters that we make use of the gifts God has given us; it matters that we work toward the vision of the peaceable reign."[13]

Work in the Spirit can be taken too far if we worship our individual work when we are doing "God's work." Dr. Jensen alludes to this in his book, *Responsive Labor*: "Work on behalf of God's reign can easily be twisted into labor for one's own self-justification and privilege."[14] It is God whom we worship, not our work. Our work is transformative, both individually and externally, but our work should always glorify God, not the worker.

What are the values of the new creation that Christian workers should emulate? Paul describes them like this:

10. Volf, *Work in the Spirit*, 100.
11. Fox, *Reinvention of Work*, 113–14 (emphasis his).
12. Volf, *Work in the Spirit*, 81 (emphasis his).
13. Jensen, *Responsive Labor*, 65 (emphasis his).
14. Jensen, *Responsive Labor*, 21.

By contrast, the fruit of the Spirit is love, joy, peace, patience, kindness, generosity, faithfulness, gentleness, and self-control. There is no law against such things. And those who belong to Christ Jesus have crucified the flesh with its passions and desires. If we live by the Spirit, let us also be guided by the Spirit. Let us not become conceited, competing against one another, envying one another. (Gal 5:22–26)

This is how Christians should work toward the new creation using their individual gifts within community. Imagine the new creation for a minute. It is a world without crime, murder, war, famine, or hostility. It is a world where people freely share and love one another within community. It is a world of respect and compassion. It is a world that worships the glory of God. It is a world where there are no boundaries, and communities work together cooperatively as one seamless world community. It is a world where all are honored equally, as all are created in God's image. It is a world at peace, and joy is found resting in God. Each one of us has a vision of the new creation, a vision that unites rather than divides. We should be striving toward this world in our work. Christians have seen it in Christ, but it is not here yet.

In practical terms, how do we know if our work is taking a step toward the new creation? Let's review again Volf's three normative principles. First, are your actions "guarding the individual's dignity" through the use of the fruit of the Spirit values? Second, are you "practicing solidarity" within community? And third, are you "preserving the integrity of nature" for future generations to steward? As Volf reminds us: people, communities, and nature are not mere things, but God's creation.[15] If you can answer these three questions positively, then you are working in the Spirit toward the new creation. Volf's questions are not a function of the type of occupations in which one works, nor the hierarchical level one achieves. Self-actualization is not about achieving personal success, although it may happen. Self-actualization is realizing your unique gifts that were created by God. The new creation balances self-actualization and community. Jesus says it best: "But strive first for the kingdom of God and his righteousness, and all these things will be given to you as well" (Matt 6:33).

The theological model of work is now developed, and Christians are called to balance the three aspects—self-actualization, community, and new creation.

15. Volf, *Work in the Spirit*, 15–16.

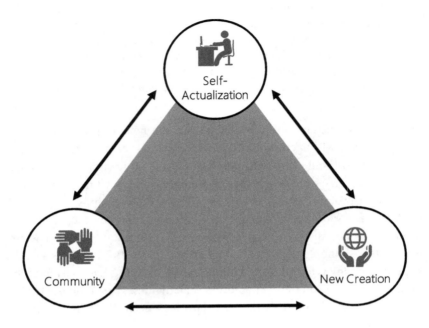

Figure 14—Theological Model of Work

Part III presents practical applications for working Christians and is organized into seven steps that build on the theological model of work.

PART III

7 Steps to Integrate Your Faith into Your Work

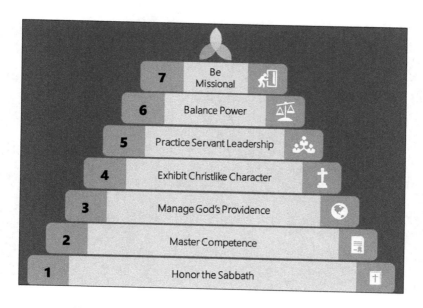

Figure 15—7 Steps to Integrate Your Faith into Your Work

Step 1: Honor the Sabbath

> *Remember the Sabbath day and keep it holy. Take a*
> *day to remove yourself from the world of space and*
> *rest in God's eternal world.*

Shabbat is needed now more than ever. We Jews should be *missionary* about
Shabbat. It may be the best gift we have to offer the world.[1]

—*Rabbi Arthur Green, Irving Brudnick Professor of*
Philosophy and Religion, Hebrew College (Boston)

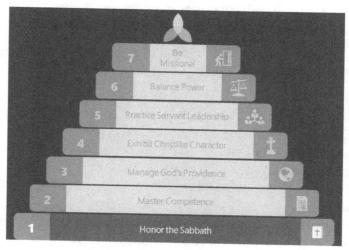

Figure 16—Step 1: Honor the Sabbath

1. Green, *Judaism's 10 Best Ideas*, 40–41 (emphasis his).

Several years ago, my wife came home from her Bible study class and asked me, "Why don't Christians observe the Sabbath?" She joined my Christian church about ten years ago and was reading the Bible with fresh eyes. I was the supposed "authority" in the family, and the question caught me off guard. I couldn't answer in a rational way. She wondered why this was the only commandment that was never really discussed. She was right.

At that time, I was part of the majority of Christians who weren't committed to observing the Sabbath. Religious writers were commenting on this. According to American Old Testament scholar Dr. Walter Brueggemann, "for the most part, contemporary Christians pay little attention to the Sabbath."[2] John Parmiter, author of *Ten at Work*, agrees:

> That the Sabbath has such a low priority is understandable. For many it is associated with dreary Sunday services and lists of prohibitions . . . If the positive value of the Sabbath is missing, especially while humankind has been looking more and more to be entertained, it is hardly surprising that people have found Sundays boring.[3]

But the Bible directs us:

> Remember the sabbath day, and keep it holy. Six days you shall labor and do all your work. But the seventh day is a sabbath to the Lord your God; you shall not do any work—you, your son or your daughter, your male or female slave, your livestock, or the alien resident in your towns. For in six days the Lord made heaven and earth, the sea, and all that is in them, but rested the seventh day; therefore the Lord blessed the sabbath day and consecrated it. (Exod 20:8–11)

In a seminary course on world religions, as part of our study of Judaism, we read *The Sabbath* by Abraham Joshua Heschel (1907–1972), an American rabbi and Jewish theologian. The beauty and the wisdom of this small book amazed me, and I asked my wife to read it. She then bought copies for her Christian women's group, and the book became a topic of discussion at our church.

Heschel's Hasidic heritage and beliefs enabled him to craft his Sabbath theology, which emphasized the realm of time over materialism. He wrote, "The meaning of the Sabbath is to celebrate time rather than space. Six days

2. Brueggemann, *Sabbath as Resistance*, ix.

3. Parmiter, *Ten at Work*, 128.

a week we live under the tyranny of things of space; on the Sabbath we try to become attuned to *holiness in time*."[4]

Heschel taught humanity that the Sabbath is at the core of Jewish holiness—that it is one of "three aspects of holiness: the holiness of the Name of God, the holiness of the Sabbath, and the holiness of Israel."[5] The Sabbath is the one day of the week when humanity can unite against the world of space and focus on something greater than space—time. It is a day away from the natural struggles of life, progress, and existence. "The Sabbath is the day on which we learn the art of *surpassing* civilization."[6]

Torah Sabbath

In Genesis, we read:

> And on the seventh day God finished the work that he had done, and he rested on the seventh day from all the work that he had done. So God blessed the seventh day and hallowed it, because on it God rested from all the work that he had done in creation. (Gen 2:2–3)

Dr. Michael Satlow, professor of Religious and Judaic Studies at Brown University, writes:

> In the Torah, observance of the Sabbath (Shabbat) is a form of *imitatio dei*, an imitation of God's cessation from labor after six days of creation. But the biblical meaning of Shabbat is far from clear. It is also God's day; like the Temple (God's house), Shabbat "belongs" to God."[7]

But Sabbath observance didn't begin until the exodus from Egypt, since the Hebrew slaves didn't rest from their labors; they were forced to gather straw after making bricks all day for Pharaoh. The exodus marks a decisive turning point in the history of the chosen people and serves as a reminder of who led them out of Egyptian slavery: "I am the Lord your God, who brought you out of the land of Egypt, out of the house of slavery; you shall have no other gods before me" (Exod 20:2–3). Dr. Brueggemann writes, "The Sabbath commandment is drawn into the exodus narrative, for the

4. Heschel, *Sabbath*, 10 (emphasis his).
5. Heschel, *Sabbath*, 81–82.
6. Heschel, *Sabbath*, 27 (emphasis his).
7. Satlow, *Creating Judaism*, 171.

God who rests is the God who emancipates *from slavery* and consequently *from the work system of Egypt* and *from the gods of Egypt* who require and legitimate that work system."[8] Sabbath is freedom from the perpetual slavery of work and focuses on obedience to the God of creation and rest.

Today, humans are caught in the constant struggle between acquiring things and living by faith that God will provide. Before Sinai, the Israelites wandered in the wilderness. God provided for their physical needs and commanded a Sabbath day of rest:

> He [Moses] said to them [leaders of the congregation], "This is what the Lord has commanded: 'Tomorrow is a day of solemn rest, a holy sabbath to the Lord; bake what you want to bake and boil what you want to boil, and all that is left over put aside to be kept until morning'" (Exod 16:23).

Even though God provided, the ancient Israelites did not always follow God's commandments or believe in God's providence, and this sometimes led to negative consequences. Today is no different from biblical times. Materialism and the constant stream of advertising are pushing humanity to acquire more space. The Sabbath causes humanity to pause the pursuit of material goods and acknowledge the giver.[9]

The positioning of the fourth commandment (Sabbath) is no accident. In the first three commandments, God spoke about God's exclusiveness. The Sabbath is a day when our thoughts are focused on God and not our own works. Rest provides a day detached from space. In the commandments that follow, God spoke about the relationship with our neighbor. The Sabbath is not celebrated alone but in community, and thus has a shared ecumenical foundation. The Sabbath serves as a fulcrum between looking up to God and turning to our neighbors as equals.

The Sabbath is central to Judaism. Dr. Roy Branson wrote, "For Heschel, celebration of the Sabbath must be the center of Judaism; for him, Sabbath was a time when disputes over concepts and deeds could be transcended by feeling with God the joy that God feels."[10] The final day of creation was not the creation of human beings, but the Sabbath. God certainly made humans in God's image and assigned humanity the stewardship of the earth, but it is the Sabbath where all praise God's glory and feel the joy

---

8. Brueggemann, *Sabbath as Resistance*, 2 (emphasis his).

9. Brueggemann, *Sabbath as Resistance*, 45.

10. Branson, "Sabbath," 732.

in God's creation.[11] This then sparks the question, "Why don't the majority of Christians observe the sabbath day and keep it holy?" The initial answer to this question is revealed during early Christianity.

Christianity and the Sabbath

Christianity and Judaism meet at the Sabbath. Early Christians did celebrate the Sabbath, since Christianity developed out of Judaism. Church historian Dr. Justo González writes, "Christians in Jerusalem continued to keep the Sabbath and attend worship at the Temple. To this they added the observance of the first day of the week, in which they gathered to break bread in celebration of the resurrection of Jesus."[12] The New Testament speaks of the Sabbath rest. Jesus observed the Sabbath and argued Jewish law with the Pharisees about the meaning of the Sabbath. He said, "For the Son of Man is lord of the sabbath," (Matt 12:8) and "The sabbath was made for humankind, and not humankind for the sabbath; so the Son of Man is lord even of the sabbath" (Mark 2:27–28).

In the Letter to the Hebrews, the Sabbath command is made more explicit:

> So then, a sabbath rest still remains for the people of God; for those who enter God's rest also cease from their labors as God did from his. Let us therefore make every effort to enter that rest, so that no one may fall through such disobedience as theirs. (Heb 4:9–11)

Book 7 of the Apostolic Constitution (about 375 CE) includes Sabbath prayers used by Christians:

> Lord, almighty, you created the world . . . and set apart the Sabbath to remember this—because on it you rested from (your) works . . . You gave them the Law of ten oracles clearly expressed by your voice and written by your hand. You commanded (them) to keep the Sabbath . . . (This is) so that men may have no excuse to plead ignorance. On account of this you entrusted (them) to keep every Sabbath that no one may desire to send forth a word from his mouth in anger on the day of the Sabbath.[13]

---

11. Moltmann, *God in Creation*, 31.

12. González, *Story of Christianity*, 1:27.

13. Jaffee, *Early Judaism*, 203–4.

The influence of the Jewish Christians centered in Jerusalem began to wane with the early Christian missionary growth through the conversions of the gentiles. Their influences were greatly reduced when the Romans destroyed the Jerusalem Temple in 70 CE and dispersed the Jews. Over time, Christians and Jews divided, especially when Christianity became the religion of the state. The delinkage continued into contemporary time. However, I advocate that Christianity must return to our Jewish Sabbath foundations.[14] It is important to remember that the Christian Sunday is not the Sabbath, as it confuses the two distinctly different days.[15] The Sabbath is a commandment, a blessed and holy day of rest. The Lord's Day (Sunday) celebrates the resurrection of Jesus Christ, a day that Judaism does not celebrate. Having two different holy days during the modern week seems rather impractical. Observing the Sabbath from Friday evening to Saturday evening followed by Sunday morning services would prove most difficult for our current society that is already rejecting Sunday as a day of rest.

John Calvin and the Sabbath

John Calvin based his work theology around Genesis 3:17–19 and believed that God made man to work, which became known as the Protestant work ethic. Calvin was so focused on removing superstition from Christianity that he lost sight of the benefits of rest. This is understandable given his difficult theological debates with the Roman Catholic Church, but the end result was the creation of an unbalanced Protestant work ethic. Calvin wrote, "It being expedient to overthrow superstition, the Jewish holy day was abolished; and as a thing necessary to retain decency, order, and peace in the church, another day was appointed for that purpose."[16]

So, according to Calvin, what is the purpose of the fourth commandment—"a sabbath to the Lord your God?" In *Institutes*, Calvin lists three purposes for the Sabbath. First, it is a day of spiritual rest where individuals "cease from their own works, and allow God to work in them." Second, it is a day people gather to be "trained to piety," through study, rites, and prayer. And third, it allows for servants to have a day of rest.[17] Calvin decided, for the sake of good order, to first "assemble on stated days for the hearing

14. Moltmann, *God in Creation*, 295–96.
15. Moltmann, *God in Creation*, 294.
16. Calvin, *Institutes of the Christian Religion*, 253.
17. Calvin, *Institutes of the Christian Religion*, 250.

of the word, the breaking of the mystical bread, and public prayer; and, secondly, to give our servants and laborers relaxation from labor."[18] Calvin described the Sabbath as a "shadowy ceremony"[19] and desired that Christians be spiritual all seven days of the week. He was driven to remove from Christianity those traditions imposed by the Catholic Church that were not supported by Scripture, and he viewed the Sabbath as "carnal superstition of sabbatism."[20]

I find that Calvin lacked an understanding of Judaism's Sabbath theology. Calvin *does* support the other nine commandments, so it defies scriptural logic when he steers away from the fourth. Had he lived to see the impact of the Industrial Age on the spiritual lives of laborers in bondage to their work, he might have delved deeper into the day of rest and reconsidered why God created the fourth commandment and why it is so necessary to observe it.

Karl Barth—Revisiting the Sabbath

As I discussed in the previous part on theology, Karl Barth begins his theology of work using Genesis and God's Holy Day. Barth's theological premise is that rest is prioritized over work. It limits human activities.[21] Humankind was created on the sixth day and, on the first day after their creation, instead of working, they rested with God. The Sabbath gave creation a "breathing space,"[22] a day where humanity acknowledges the Lord of creation.

A practical theological model of work must place "honoring the Sabbath" as a foundational attribute. Without resting in God one day of the week, working Christians' priorities are not aligned with obedience to God's Sabbath commandment. Christian life becomes unbalanced and the secular world dominates. Space dominates all the days of our lives.

18. Calvin, *Institutes of the Christian Religion*, 252.
19. Calvin, *Institutes of the Christian Religion*, 253.
20. Calvin, *Institutes of the Christian Religion*, 253.
21. Barth, *Doctrine of Creation*, 3:50.
22. Barth, *Doctrine of Creation*, 3:52.

Judaism's Struggles with the Sabbath

Like Christianity, Judaism struggles with how to observe the Sabbath in our modern world. A range of practices abound in Judaism, just as in Christianity. Dr. Michael Satlow proposes: "Shabbat is a time for study, family and community renewal, play, and restraint from work . . . Each individual is empowered to make his or her own decision, although that decision would ideally be made within the framework of the tradition."[23] This rational approach to the Sabbath should make sense to the Christian community as a means of returning to the Sabbath. One's spiritual life has no room to grow when seven days per week are a perpetual treadmill of human activities. Resting is actually a gift, a way to enjoy life and honor God. Without this rest, we are a slave to human work and cultural expectations which leads to burnout. "Sabbath is therefore a *declaration of our freedom*."[24]

A Return to the Sabbath

I grew up during the 1960s and 1970s in south Texas. From Monday through Saturday, we went to work or school, performed household duties, and bought household items. My parents were both Christian, and we regularly attended Sunday morning worship, Sunday school, and Sunday evening church activities. We did not observe the Sabbath as a stated value, but Sunday was a family day with a special noon meal and rest from the normal weekday activities. We did no household or commercial chores, although my mother worked to prepare the noon meal. Almost all businesses were closed due to the Texas Blue Laws and the influence of Christian churches. Normally, TV was not allowed on Sundays, as it was also a school night. Of course, there were no computers or mobile phones. Community sports were not played on Sundays. In many ways, we observed most aspects of the Sabbath without specifically naming it. Our community structure created a day of rest, as there was little else to do but rest in time.

I moved my family to London in 1994, and this great commercial city practically shut down on Sundays. People stayed home with their families and rested. Pubs, which were community gathering places, closed after the traditional Sunday roast meal. We traveled to Germany during December 1995 for a week of vacation and found that all stores closed from Saturday

23. Satlow, *Creating Judaism*, 41.
24. Keller, *Every Good Endeavor*, 243–44 (emphasis his).

noon until Monday morning. We were warned, so we traveled with food and cooked in our apartment. We just relaxed with the family, attended church services, and took afternoon family walks.

By 2004, when moving to the Netherlands, I noticed that stores and restaurants were open on Sunday. Along with other European countries, this previously "Calvinist" society was becoming more secular and less observant of the Sabbath.

Today, Sunday is like any other day of the week for most Americans and Europeans. Stores usually open a few hours later, but most commercial operations have a lively Sunday business. Parents spend their weekends carting their children to various activities, and sporting events are in full swing. Except for my Sunday morning church attendance, Sunday is not very different from any other day of the week. It has become a day of space.

Yet, I yearn for the Sabbath. I long for my childhood days of rest and focus on time, not space. We recently traveled to the South Pacific Islands, which were Christianized during the early nineteenth century. Most communities were structured around a small church, and the Sabbath was observed. These formerly non-Christian communities gave me hope that perhaps the Anglo-Christian communities that brought the Sabbath to these small islands could again honor it.

Now is the time to return to the Sabbath and reclaim the celebration that Judaism never lost. The bonds of the Jewish community that center on the Sabbath will enrich Christianity and provide an ecumenical platform for reconciliation, which is long overdue. All people should journey together spiritually, and the Sabbath is a starting point.

A Proposed Path Toward Honoring the Sabbath

Using Dr. Arthur Green's *Ten Pathways toward a New Shabbat*[25] as an outline, I propose these simple rules for a Christian Sabbath:

1. Spend Sabbath (Sunday or another day each week) at home with family. Start by lighting candles, one for each member present, at the beginning of the Sabbath meal. Say a special blessing, giving thanks to God for the Sabbath, creation, and community. Sabbath meals should be simple, practical, and prepared in advance, so all may rest in community.

25. Green, *Judaism's 10 Best Ideas*, 44–46.

2. Worship as a family in community.

3. Read something that challenges you—something you're not reading during the other six days of the week. Read for contemplation and not as a task.

4. Spend some time in personal prayer and spiritual meditation. Reflect on your past week, both positively and constructively.

5. Don't conduct any vocational work, such as physical tasks, emails, work readings, presentations, analysis, etc. Avoid unnecessary household chores.

6. Don't spend money on the Sabbath. This includes shopping, paying bills, and calling commercial organizations.

7. Don't use the Internet or computer during the Sabbath. Spend the day in face-to-face conversations or video linkage to connect with distant family and friends.

8. Don't travel on the Sabbath. Stay away from airports, rental cars, hotel check-ins and restaurants. If you're away, observe Sabbath as if you were at home, if at all possible.

9. Don't watch TV or home entertainment alone. Play with the family or bond with your spouse and friends.

10. End Sabbath as a family by saying a special prayer and extinguishing the Sabbath candles.

Of course, these simple rules are suggestions, and you should adjust them to your family situation. When I get invitations to dine out on Sundays with friends, I usually accept them, as relationship and community trump the desire to avoid spending money on the Sabbath. If I'm on vacation and traveling with friends, I don't impractically impose my Sabbath rules on them if they are not observant. Being somewhat flexible rather than absolutely rigid allows for experiencing life's special events and building relationships. However, Sabbaths are for resting in God and allowing others to do the same. It must be a weekly priority.

The Sabbath is a time for celebration, not anger, bitterness, or mourning. According to the Bible, "You shall kindle no fire in all your dwellings on the sabbath day" (Exod 35:3). This also applies to the mind, heart, and soul, as well as physical work. As Heschel wrote, it is impossible to rest in God without *shalom*: "The Sabbath, thus, is more than an armistice, more than an interlude; it is a profound conscious harmony of man and the world."[26]

How do we stop work when the secular world calls for people to do more to gain additional material possessions? Why are we so afraid of having leisure time without checking off another task on our to-do list? In my younger days, when my spouse and I had professional jobs and were raising two children, Sunday after church was more a time to get ready for another workweek than rest. I did household chores, bought groceries, and shopped at the mall. I never thought about relaxing, as I viewed leisure time as wasteful (the Protestant work ethic) unless there was a family gathering, community event, or special sporting event.

It's time for Christianity to go back to its earliest days and listen again to Jewish wisdom. God gave humans six days to work and, in God's infinite wisdom, instructed us to rest, worship, and bond with our neighbors on the seventh day. Being idle while resting in God on the Sabbath does feel pretty good once you try it. Rabbi Heschel says it best:

> There is a realm of time where the goal is not to have but to be, not to own but to give, not to control but to share, not to subdue but to be in accord. Life goes wrong when the control of space, the acquisition of things of space, becomes our sole concern.[27]

26. Heschel, *Sabbath*, 31.
27. Heschel, *Sabbath*, 3.

Step 2: Master Competence

> *Be proficient at a skill by working hard*
> *and long to master it.*
> *Be competent in your religion, a faith*
> *seeking understanding.*

If you are called to be a street sweeper, sweep streets as Michelangelo painted or Beethoven composed music or Shakespeare wrote poetry.
Sweep streets so well that all the hosts of heaven and earth will pause to say, Here lived a great sweeper who did his job well.[1]

—*MARTIN LUTHER KING, JR.*

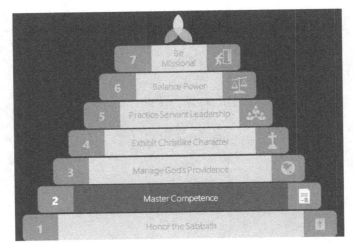

Figure 17—Step 2: Master Competence

1. Shattock, *Wake Up to Work*, 39.

IN 1976, I ENTERED the Colorado School of Mines (CSM), an engineering university in Golden, which had a good reputation in the energy profession. I'd enjoyed my high school math and science courses, and I wanted a job with an energy company like my father, who was a geologist with Exxon. I'd always wanted to live in the mountains after spending most of my childhood near the warm and breezy Texas Gulf Coast. After backpacking as a Boy Scout at Philmont Scout Ranch in northern New Mexico, I was hooked on the dry, cool mountain air. I was a good (but not great) high school student, and I also enjoyed the social life, church fellowship, and extracurricular activities. My grades were good enough to get into the engineering school of my choice, and I wanted to explore and enjoy the Rocky Mountains during my college years.

Soon after my arrival at CSM, I quickly realized that high school and college courses were quite different! Engineering school demanded much more time, and the scholastic competition was much greater. I struggled the first year due to my lack of preparation, since my high school hadn't offered Advanced Placement courses. I passed all my classes, but my grades were lower than in high school, and I wasn't proud of my initial college accomplishments.

When I returned to CSM for my second year after working as a roustabout in the California desert, I knew I wanted to be a chemical engineer, and that meant taking many chemistry courses. In my first hour-long exam in Physical Chemistry III, I received a failing grade. I had never failed an exam in my life, and this was in my major. I was shocked and depressed. I decided to drop the class, as I did not want to risk having a failed class on my transcript. I did some soul-searching and decided that this event would not define me. I asked my professor if I could stay in the class and audit it. He agreed.

I continued to attend class and do the homework. I decided that I needed to work harder, so each night, I studied at the library until it closed. I decided to study until I knew the course material completely. After each lecture, I organized my notes before reading the textbook. I networked with older students who had taken these classes. They shared their class materials and exams for me to review and practice. I worked all problem sets until I obtained the correct solution, and I asked for help when I needed it. I also worked on increasing the speed of my calculations to maximize my testing abilities. As painful as it was, I became much more disciplined, and my grades dramatically improved that semester.

The next semester, I took Physical Chemistry III again. I was the first to turn in my exam, in less than the allotted hour. I received the highest grade on that exam and also for the entire course. I learned a great life lesson: to succeed in life, one must master competence, and this requires hard, disciplined work.

When I graduated, after learning the importance of discipline and competence, I had a number of job offers. Once employed, I had to face the reality that my peers had *also* graduated at the top of excellent engineering universities and most had more professional experience than I did. In addition, the problems were more complex and no longer had defined answers. I had to make assumptions and develop the data, then decide on the correct application. The corporation invested in my development by sending me to technical schools and assigning mentors. Each day, my performance was judged through the watchful eyes of my supervisor, colleagues, and senior managers.

Mastering competence never stopped for the next thirty-four years of my working life. Each increasingly challenging assignment and promotion presented new problems, which meant I had to constantly learn and adapt. Those who were not continually learning new skills did not compete well in a changing environment. As I advanced in management, the people at the higher levels were all highly intelligent, disciplined, and fast learners. To be effective, I had to master competence again and again.

Ken Costa, a senior UK investment banker and chairman of Alpha International, is a high achiever in both business and evangelism. In his book, *God at Work*, he speaks about competency:

> More than ever before we need Christians with ambition in the workplace. People who will set demanding challenges for themselves but who will also recognize that true ambition cannot be achieved individually. We are to be accountable to others and hold others to account. We also need to break the perception that God prefers us to settle into being low achievers, or we will fail to make an impact on our communities.[2]

2. Costa, *God at Work*, 67.

Mastering Competence and the Theological Model

How does competency relate to the "theology of work" model? Self-actualization occurs through mastering competence. God calls all persons to use their talents, which must be developed to master competence. In the parable of the talents (Matt 25:14–30), Jesus tells the story of a man who entrusted his property to his servants; the servant who did not productively use his skills was punished: "For to all those who have, more will be given, and they will have an abundance; but from those who have nothing, even what they have will be taken away" (Matt 25:29). William Diehl, a former sales manager for Bethlehem Steel and author of *The Monday Connection*, explains the relationship between faith and competence. These dedicated Christians—"composers, writers, artists, educators, political leaders, scientists, physicians"—"were extraordinarily competent in their work." Christians give glory to God by striving "to do our absolute best."[3]

First, our skills and talents are God-given. When we refine them, we shine inwardly from our proficiencies, but we also know that the glory goes to God the creator from whom the skills originated. Dr. Larive, a professor and a carpenter, writes that "only a very vain person gives himself sole credit for a skill, because a skill seems so much like a gift—something one feels pleased and fortunate to have."[4]

Second, mastering competence bolsters the community. Christians are called to enhance and support their communities through their God-given skills. Self-actualization is balanced through community. We are called to serve, and the best way to serve our community is by being highly proficient at our skill. While we may believe strongly that it was only our hard work and talents that resulted in our success, in reality, success was achieved through community mentoring and opportunities. "Therefore, everything you have is a matter of grace, and so *you have the freedom to serve the world through your influence*, just as you can through your competence."[5]

Third, the skills required to create a better future will be increasingly more complex and will require Christians to be constant learners as information and technologies rapidly expand. In moving toward the new creation, good stewardship requires mastering competence and following the Spirit, which helps to sustain workers. Miroslav Volf writes that the Spirit

3. Diehl, *Monday Connection*, 45.

4. Larive, *After Sunday*, 110–11.

5. Keller, *Every Good Endeavor*, 120; emphasis mine.

imparts various gifts to workers. "These gifts form part of their personality that they are responsible to respect and to develop, both because of the intrinsic value of their personalities as integral parts of the new creation, and because the more they are developed, the better they can anticipate the new creation through their work."[6]

Working Hard and Long

Working hard to master competence is not enough. We must be disciplined, loyal to a profession, and gain expertise through failures and struggles before becoming proficient. When success is achieved, the external world sees the triumph, but usually does not see the years of struggle, constant failures, and internal questioning. Angela Duckworth, author of *Grit: The Power of Passion and Perseverance*, writes about a discussion she had with a Wharton business student. The student was an entrepreneur who worked incredibly hard to successfully raise money for a start-up. But the student did not understand that hard work alone was not enough. There are no shortcuts to obtain competency:

> "Grit isn't *just* working incredibly hard. That's only part of it."
>
> Pause.
>
> "Why?"
>
> "Well, for one thing, there are no shortcuts to excellence. Developing real expertise, figuring out really hard problems, it all takes time—longer than most people imagine. And then, you know, you've got to apply those skills and produce goods or services that are valuable to people. Rome wasn't built in a day."
>
> He was listening, so I continued.
>
> "And here's the really important thing. Grit is about working on something you care about so much that you're willing to stay loyal to it."
>
> "It's doing what you love. I get that."
>
> "Right, it's doing what you love, but not just falling in love—*staying* in love."[7]

Becoming competent in a profession requires a passion toward excellence in the face of major challenges. To succeed in engineering school, I had to spend much more time and energy than I initially thought I would.

---

6. Volf, *Work in the Spirit*, 173.

7. Duckworth, *Grit*, 53–54.

Until I was confident that I could immediately answer any exam question without having to ponder or struggle, I kept working to master the skill. I could no longer accept mediocrity. As professor Duckworth points out, "experts do it all over again, and again, and again." Through the struggle, expertise is developed "until conscious incompetence becomes unconscious competence."[8]

The church has long struggled with articulating the need for mastering competence in secular professions. In fact, I can't remember ever hearing a sermon or church discussion on the subject. In her book *Creed or Chaos?*, English writer and expert in classical languages Dorothy Sayers (1893–1957) wrote about the church's failure "to understand and respect the secular vocation." The church has separated work and religion to the detriment of workers. Instead of telling workers that they should be sober and orderly church goers (an important message), a more relevant message is that workers should be competent.[9]

Mastering Religious Competence

Mastering competence does not reside solely in the secular world. Once a Christian accepts Christ through faith, the discipleship journey continues throughout life. As previously discussed, theology is *faith seeking understanding*. Christians are called to be competent in their faith by reading Scripture, hearing the word, attending community discipleship classes, and reading Christian articles and books. Christians do not need to go to seminary to become competent in their faith, but they do need to continually grow in knowledge and understanding. Discipleship is a lifelong journey toward mastering Christian competence.

When I went to seminary to earn my Master's degree, I hadn't been in a graduate school for twenty-eight years. I knew that my technical and business background would be little help in seminary. My writing and reading comprehension skills would have to improve. I realized I would need to quickly acquire new skills to begin to master theological competence.

Most of my fellow seminary students desired to become pastors, which are teaching elders. Congregations look to their pastors to be their teachers through preaching, teaching, leading, and counseling. This requires mastering competence, just like in secular professions. Congregations have

8. Duckworth, *Grit*, 123.
9. Sayers, *Creed or Chaos*, 106–7.

a right to demand that their pastors be highly competent in theological studies.

I noticed that some members of the class did not have adequate time to commit to their studies. In some cases, they were starting a second career as a pastor and had families to support, so they needed to work part-time. Some had spouses who needed to remain in another city to work, which made for stressful long-distance commutes and relationships. The reading load, papers, and exam preparation time for full-time students required a full-time commitment to master competence. Some students viewed seminary simply as a checklist to get into church work. I did not question their commitment to Christ nor their love for the church. What I did question was how they were going to lead their congregations if they had not mastered their religious studies?

When I took my second semester of theology, the course was taught by a visiting professor who was an excellent teacher. His lectures were always organized and informative, but he would not give students the answers. He expected us to read the theological texts and condense each theologian's beliefs into a well-constructed, concise three-page paper. Several students complained to the seminary administration that the course was too difficult. While I was studying in the dining area one day, the professor walked in and sat down next to me. I was surprised, as he had never spoken to me one-to-one except when I asked questions.

He said that he noticed me in class because I was always alert and focused on the lectures. I told him that the theologians we studied were difficult to understand, and I struggled through the many assigned readings to capture their concepts. But once I finally grasped their theology, it was a joyful moment as the theologian either resonated with my beliefs or helped me understand a different view. The professor told me about some students' complaints and asked my opinion. I spoke openly: "Don't give in as life after seminary will not have 'fill-in-the-blank' answers. If the students don't learn to struggle with the readings to master competence in their religious studies, they won't be able to fully answer questions from their congregations. They won't be *fluent* in their profession."

The professor smiled and thanked me. He did not downgrade the course and stood his ground. Most people remember teachers who were tough, yet fair, and stretched their students toward mastering competence.

An Old Testament Example—Daniel

In the Old Testament, Daniel was an example of mastering competence in the workplace. King Darius I of Persia saw Daniel's workplace performance and decided to promote him:

> Soon Daniel distinguished himself above all the other presidents and satraps because an excellent spirit was in him, and the king planned to appoint him over the whole kingdom. (Dan 6:3)

Mastering competence sometimes comes at a personal cost, as Daniel's fellow managers became jealous and worked to remove him, even though Daniel was innocent:

> So the presidents and the satraps tried to find grounds for complaint against Daniel in connection with the kingdom. But they could find no grounds for complaint or any corruption, because he was faithful, and no negligence or corruption could be found in him. The men said, "We shall not find any ground for complaint against this Daniel unless we find it in connection with the law of his God." So the presidents and satraps conspired . . . .(Dan 6:4–6)

King Darius eventually realized that Daniel was innocent, and he prospered after his workplace challenges. This story shows the value of mastering competence.

Even mastering competence does not mean that a worker will never have challenges, face rival politics, or experience disappointments. These are just part of the journey of faith. But with expertise, knowledge, and proficient skills, a faithful worker can strive toward obtaining self-actualization, building community, and stepping closer to the new creation. During the journey of faith, we must always give thanks to God who created us and our learned skills. We are blessed, so we return thanks. David Jensen says this so well when he writes that good work is a blessing from God for which the worker responds in thanksgiving:

> Good work, in and of itself, is an expression of thanks: a finely crafted chair, a graceful gymnastics routine, a sound medical diagnosis, a brightly waxed car, all involve work that employs gifts and gives thanks for them. Indeed, as an expression of thanks, the work of our hands often speaks more clearly and distinctly than our words.[10]

10. Jensen, *Responsive Labor*, 92–93.

Step 3: Manage God's Providence

> *God provides, and we are God's stewards on earth. Manage God's resources effectively and benevolently within your workplace, home, and church.*

Gain all you can, without hurting either yourself or your neighbour, in soul or body, by applying hereto with unintermitted diligence, and with all the understanding which God has given you.

Save all you can, by cutting off every expense which serves only to indulge foolish desire, to gratify either the desire of the flesh, the desire of the eye, or the pride of life.

Waste nothing, living or dying, on sin or folly, whether for yourself or your children.

And then, *Give all you can*, or in other words give all you have to God.[1]

—*REV. JOHN WESLEY, FOUNDER OF METHODISM*

Moreover, it is God's gift that all should eat and drink and take pleasure in all their toil.

—*ECCLESIASTES 3:13*

1. Wesley, *John Wesley's Sermons*, 356 (emphasis his).

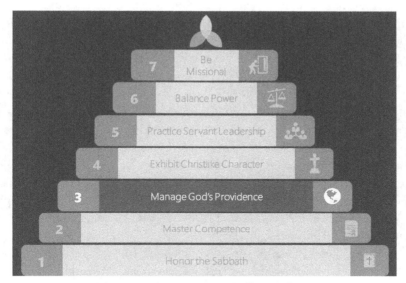

Figure 18—Step 3: Manage God's Providence

MY LAST WORK ASSIGNMENT before retirement was with Shell Energy Europe. I was the general manager of the Northwest Region, managing Shell's gas/power trading and marketing business. Since my wife also worked in the same office building on the Strand just north of the Thames River, we would walk together for thirty minutes through central London to our offices. My favorite time to make this walk was in the early morning because the pedestrian traffic was lighter and the low sun, when it was not raining, cast beautiful light on the stately British buildings.

Family and friends who stayed with us in our central London location said that we lived the good life. They were correct, in one sense. We lived as corporate ex-pats in a wonderful international city and had the means to enjoy our time in Europe. After work, we would decide whether to buy food to cook that evening or pop into a small restaurant for our evening meal. On weekends, we would regularly rent a car and drive into the English countryside or take Saturday day trips by train to explore British cities outside London. Long weekends were usually spent traveling to other European cities. We often went to plays and operas. Many Sunday afternoons were spent taking walks through the lovely London parks. We were grateful for God's providence.

After more than four years in London, we made the decision to retire and build a home in central Austin. Three months later, I entered seminary. I felt that if I did not immediately go back to school and complete my Master of Theology degree, I would get bogged down in other projects or convince myself that it was just too much effort to return to graduate school.

Early in my first semester of classes, my assignment was to write a three-page personal sermon founded on one of John Wesley's sermons. I sought advice from Jim, a retired United Methodist minister, because I had limited knowledge of Wesley's sermons. He suggested that I read *The Use of Money*, although he said it was difficult. Perhaps he also thought it would be a teachable moment for me. The sermon was indeed transformational, and it changed my thinking on possessions and money. Wesley summed up his theology on money with a simple phrase: *gain* all you can, *save* all you can, and *give* all you can.

I asked Jim for feedback on my rough draft. He kindly obliged and returned it with his comments. Because he had previously taught Methodist studies at the seminary, he knew how to critique a paper. In the "*save* all you can" paragraphs, I wrote that Christians should consult their financial and tax advisors to be good stewards of their money. Here, Jim wrote a simple note: "Did you know that 99 percent of Americans do not have financial advisors since they do not earn enough money to justify this expense?" His statement hit squarely in my heart, as I realized that my late-career lifestyle had warped my sense of reality and I had forgotten my earlier financial struggles. Thanks to Jim's comment, I returned to earth and started to reconnect with reality.

God Provides

After first laying the foundations to *Honor the Sabbath* and *Master Competence*, the next step is to *Manage God's Providence*. My reconnection started with understanding where providence comes from and who actually owns it: the eternal God. Genesis states that God created the world and created humankind:

> God blessed them, and God said to them, "Be fruitful and multiply, and fill the earth and subdue it; and have dominion over the fish of the sea and over the birds of the air and over every living thing that moves upon the earth" (Gen 1:28).

All the world was created by God, and all is ultimately related to God. Therefore, whatever humans possess is not theirs, but God's. Humans are made in God's image and are stewards of the world. Humanity is accountable to God. Douglas Hall, professor of theology at McGill University in Canada, writes that once we realize that God owns everything and humans are "at most stewards," then suddenly the world is "thrown into a critical perspective."[2] For God owns the earth, and it is on loan for humans to take care of it:

> For every wild animal of the forest is mine, the cattle on a thousand hills.
> I know all the birds of the air, and all that moves in the field is mine.
> (Ps 50:10–11)

In 1 Corinthians 3:22–23, the New Testament continues this same theme of all belonging to God, with humans as stewards of the world: "All belong to you, and you belong to Christ, and Christ belongs to God." Dr. Douglass Hall says that stewardship is obedience to God as "faithful trustees of the life of the world."[3] Jesus understood the importance of stewardship since over half his teachings dealt with money and possessions.[4]

What we do with God's providence reflects our being and faith. Luke Timothy Johnson, American professor of New Testament at Chandler School of Theology, writes about how our possessions can interfere with "our sense of identity and worth as human beings. The real sin related to possessions has to do with the willful confusion of being and having."[5] The apostle Paul reflects on our possessions in his first letter to Timothy:

> Of course, there is great gain in godliness combined with contentment; for we brought nothing into the world, so that we can take nothing out of it; but if we have food and clothing, we will be content with these. But those who want to be rich fall into temptation and are trapped by many senseless and harmful desires that plunge people into ruin and destruction. For the love of money is a root of all kinds of evil, and in their eagerness to be rich some have wandered away from the faith and pierced themselves with many pains. (1 Tim 6:6–10)

2. Hall, *Steward*, 42.

3. Hall, *Steward*, 44.

4. Costa, *God at Work*, 161.

5. Johnson, *Sharing Possessions*, 37.

If humans see material possessions as a reflection of their being, then through their bodies and actions they deny the supremacy of God. Our possessions become idols. Johnson says, "Idolatry is found in the service of the heart, the way we concretely and existentially dispose of our freedom."[6] Christians are therefore called to a theology of poverty where being takes precedence over having. God alone calls us worthy and it is God's gift, which is unearned and cannot be bought through our own deeds: "Our being and worth come from him alone, for by ourselves we fall into nothingness at every moment."[7]

We live in a complex and constantly changing world. The United States, a country founded on freedom, is the most advanced capitalistic nation on earth. Americans make daily choices related to their material possessions. A Christian's monetary decisions reflect his or her faith. William Cavanaugh, professor of Catholic Studies at DePaul University, believes that "true freedom is not just following whatever desires we happen to have, but cultivating the right desires."[8] The United States is commonly considered a consumerist culture because we have an uncommon knack for turning anything into a commodity, something that can be bought and sold.[9] The pleasure comes not just from the possession, but from the pursuit of the material world.[10]

How do Christians put a stop to the pursuit of possessions? John Bolt, professor of Systematic Theology at Calvin Theological Seminary, has a solution: "We can choose simplicity and refuse to participate in the excesses of market idolatry. We *can* just say no!"[11] Even if we can afford it, being good stewards of God's creation may mean that we say no to a purchase. Christians are to be a "*Contrast Community* . . . It understands itself as different from the world."[12] This means that we look at the world differently from the secular community. Our being is derived from God, not from our possessions. How do we make purchasing decisions? Dr. Cavanaugh answers: If the purchase's ultimate end result reflects the image of God within

6. Johnson, *Sharing Possessions*, 48.

7. Johnson, *Sharing Possessions*, 77.

8. Cavanaugh, *Being Consumed*, 11–12.

9. Cavanaugh, *Being Consumed*, 34.

10. Cavanaugh, *Being Consumed*, 47.

11. Bolt, *Economic Shalom*, 103 (emphasis his).

12. Barrett et al., *Treasure in Clay Jars*, xiii (emphasis his).

God's creation, then Christians can feel comfortable with the transaction. "Created things are to be *used*, but only God is to be *enjoyed*."[13]

Relationship of Providence to the Theological Model of Work

Self-actualization is realized through careful management of God's providence. John Wesley first spoke about *gaining* all you can. He did not mean becoming rich, as money is not mentioned. He speaks about maximizing God-given talents "by applying hereto with unintermitted diligence, and with all the understanding which God has given you." One must work toward excellence through diligence. But Wesley follows this first statement with efficiency and discipline: *saving* all you can. Being a good steward means not wasting God's providence and leaving our planet's resources for future generations: "Waste nothing, living or dying, on sin or folly, whether for yourself or your children."[14] It is difficult to obtain self-actualization if workers misuse their resources. During my college years and through most of my professional life, I kept a strict spending budget and saved for my retirement, my children's college expenses, and the reduction of mortgage debt. There were always more wants than our budget allowed, but our basic needs were met. I was occasionally tempted, but after seeing that our long-term priorities could not be funded if we bought an item, I decided not to make the purchase. Businessman and writer John Parmiter wrote that money never satisfies. "God is not opposed to money, but he is opposed to the *worship* of it."[15] It is far more satisfying to obtain self-actualization and support community than worship money and seek riches.

Self-actualization occurs through human development. A robust economy is needed for humans to flourish and self-actualize. If people spend all their time just obtaining the basic food and water requirements, then self-actualization will not occur. However, a modern society that allows for economic growth of a few at the expense of the self-actualization of many goes directly against God's desire that everyone should be given the opportunity to achieve self-actualization.[16]

13. Cavanaugh, *Being Consumed*, 49.
14. Wesley, *John Wesley's Sermons*, 356.
15. Parmiter, *Ten at Work*, 33 (emphasis his).
16. Volf, *Work in the Spirit*, 153–54.

The pursuit of self-actualization by managing God's providence must be balanced through community. Wesley follows *"Gain all you can"* with "without hurting either yourself or your neighbour, in soul or body."[17] We live in community. Sanctification is God's love that transforms Christians to look outwardly into their community rather than just focus on self-actualization. It is understanding that God provides, and there is enough for all. Dr. Larive explains that Christians need to view the world not as economic scarcity, but that God provides enough for all to prosper. "A Christian perspective ought to see that there is enough of what is required for life and that no one should be in want while another has too much. Scarcity and insatiable wants are social constructions rather than timeless truths."[18] Jesus' parable of the Good Samaritan is a wonderful example of community and the use of our resources to assist our neighbors:

> He went to him and bandaged his wounds, having poured oil and wine on them. Then he put him on his own animal, brought him to an inn, and took care of him. The next day he took out two denarii, gave them to the innkeeper, and said, "Take care of him; and when I come back, I will repay you whatever more you spend." (Luke 10:34–35)

Wesley's final statement, *"Give all you can,"* had community in mind. He followed this statement with "or in other words, give all you have to God." He did not mean that God needed your resources, as our God who created the world does not need our trivial resources. Giving to God means being good stewards and using our resources to improve the community. When working with God's providence, workers are required to use God's resources to uplift their communities. According to Costa, "generous giving is liberating." Giving frees us from dependence on our possessions and the powerful hold of money. "What we cannot give freely, possesses us. Giving is the antidote to materialism.[19]

Self-actualization and community must be placed in balance with the new creation. Managing God's providence is a multi-generational process, as our individual time on earth is limited. Being good stewards requires Christians to maintain the earth for future generations. Christianity does not advocate an economic system, but it does advocate an economy that

---

17. Wesley, *John Wesley's Sermons*, 356 (emphasis his).

18. Larive, *After Sunday*, 140.

19. Costa, *God at Work*, 171.

uses resources effectively while being good stewards of the environment.[20] No matter what economic system is employed, the Holy Spirit focuses Christians on the new creation. "Those who have experienced the power of the Holy Spirit cannot be indifferent to the destruction of the nonhuman creation."[21]

Consumer Choices

How is "managing God's providence" put into my daily practice? I was fortunate to be born into a nonmaterialistic Protestant family. My parents were middle class and we lived comfortably, but our possessions were basic. I received what I needed, not what I wanted. Saving for children's education, participating in church life, and focusing on doing well in school were our family's priorities. Our few vacations were spent visiting relatives and learning about our country. My parents shielded me from consumerism until I left home. I did not have the struggles and unexpected financial burdens that many people experience growing up. Although I did not know of Wesley's *"save all you can"* principle during this early period of my life, I was fortunate to follow his theology. However, I could have been much less materialistic.

My income increased when I was promoted into middle management. Because of our conservative lifestyle, the extra money went into savings for retirement, and we decided to fund our grandchildren's university education. It was nice to have the income, but it did not define my being. After reading Wesley's *The Use of Money* sermon in 2014, I realized that all I had came from God. Using Matthew 25:35–36 as the criteria for giving, my wife and I decided to radically increase the giving of our time, talent, and financial resources to others. As Dr. Luke Timothy Johnson states, "To love our neighbor is to be creatively faithful to God; to show fidelity to our neighbor is to love the Lord with all our heart."[22] We are expending more time in our community and giving more financially. I am sure there is more I can do for others during my twilight years. This is something that I continually need to reflect upon and adjust.

I was blessed with an excellent career, and although the economic environment varied greatly during my thirty-plus years of professional

20. Costa, *God at Work*, 83.

21. Volf, *Work in the Spirit*, 153.

22. Johnson, *Sharing Possessions*, 97.

employment, I fortunately never lost my job—something that others have tragically experienced. Because of our conservative lifestyle, if my employment had been terminated for a period, my family had enough financial resources to survive long enough for me to find other employment, or my spouse's income would have covered our basic needs. For many Americans who have low salaries, experience medical or other hardships, or make poor decisions on their expenditures, unemployment may mean homelessness, no medical insurance, hunger, and stress. John Wesley's message to *"save all you can"* is his way of telling us to live within our means, be efficient, and if possible, save enough for future needs, like education or emergencies. Wesley gives both good financial and good theological advice. We now give joyfully and gratefully, not just dutifully and responsibly. *"Give all you can"* is the recognition that a person is not defined by their possessions. In our materialistic society, this is one of Christianity's biggest challenges.

Make Financial Decisions at Work as if the Money Is Your Own

In 1994, I accepted my first overseas assignment in London. I had never traveled to Europe until my family flew over together, and I started working in London the day after we landed. The large London office had many different operating practices than in Houston; for instance, how the company processed business expenses. In Houston, travel expenses were filed after being incurred by filling out a business expense claim for reimbursement. I submitted the claim form with my receipts, my manager approved them, and Accounting sent me the reimbursement money. I was trained on what expenses could be claimed as business expenses, and I followed the company's travel policy. In London, the travel department would calculate a per diem travel expense based on the travel location(s), where one lived and the job group level.

After I received the reimbursement for my first business trip, I realized that I had an average of £100 per day of money in my bank account over what I had spent on business expenses. I went to a British manager and asked him what I should do. He just chuckled and told me that this was a fringe benefit. He traveled frequently and optimized the per diem through several practices. First, he optimized the travel locations, as the per diem rates varied by location. Second, as the local offices in the countries that he traveled to paid for many of his meals, he was able to pocket the per diem business meal expense money. And third, he opted to take the cheaper public transportation rather than the higher-cost taxi that the per diem estimates were based on. Although this took more travel time, he kept the difference.

While the per diem business travel policy was legal under British tax law, two things bothered me personally. First, the purpose of business travel was to grow and add value to the business, not the employee. The per diem system sadly allowed employees to misuse company funds for personal gain. Second, it was wasteful. I saw many cases of unnecessary business travel, and I surmised that this travel expense policy encouraged self-serving behaviors at the expense of the company.

Wesley's "*save all you can*" theology applies to how you manage workplace finances. Since all resources come from God and humans are God's stewards on earth, we are called to wisely use all resources prudently, efficiently, and effectively. The same applies to government, university, non-profit, and corporate workers. Workplace resources that we manage should be treated as if they were our own resources: prudently, efficiently, and effectively. Eventually, the London office changed its travel expense policy and began reimbursing for actual travel expenses rather than a per diem rate.

Church Budgets are Based on Their Priorities

In the early 1990s, before I left for my first London assignment, I was a member of a Houston suburban church. I served on the Session—the elected ruling body of the church. Our church was built in 1985 in a fast-growing new Houston suburb. This community was composed of recently built homes, parks, shopping centers, churches, and golf courses.

Energy prices drove the Houston economy during this period. While I served on the Session, there was an economic recession after oil prices fell below $20 per barrel. Many people lost their jobs, or their salaries were reduced due to the decline in the energy business. It was a difficult economic time for the Houston community. My church had recently built a sanctuary, church office, fellowship hall, and an educational building. Due to the poor Houston economy, pledges fell and, in some cases, were not funded. The Session was faced with difficult financial decisions.

Our church always wanted to give more money to needy communities near and far, but after building a large church facility, adding staff, and other associated expenditures, there was little left over to serve others out-side our church membership. While we tried to annually allocate 5 percent to external missions, many times our church did not achieve the 5 percent goal. The priorities were "*gain all you can*," then *build* all you can.

Church expenses were minimized when possible, as the Session em-ployed the "*save all you can*" philosophy. In the end, the Session agreed that mission funding was already too low, but there wasn't enough money to fund missions after allocating money to previous commitments. It was decided to cut all mission funding. Our church dollars went only internally to members. I was devastated, as past Session decisions on funding internal priorities left little for external community service.

As I left that Session meeting, another member said to me, "You and I seem to be on opposite sides. I believe that *our* church money should go for *our* families, and you believe that nonchurch families should receive some of *our* hard-earned money." I was astonished, as both of us read the same Scripture and came to totally different conclusions. I replied, "Yes, you're right. We *are* on opposite sides on this issue."

I walked out of the beautiful facilities that we had built. As the Session members drove away in expensive automobiles, I viewed all the new ex-pensive suburban homes, many with swimming pools, that surrounded our church building. I surmised that our church's priorities were not aligned with the gospel. Our church's finances did reflect the church's priorities. They were directed inwardly.

I realized that our church was just another country club with a spiritu-al component. When our minister left for another church a few years later, our interim minister walked into our church building and commented, "I know where your priorities are." He didn't have to examine the church's operating budget. It was there before his eyes. This church did not "*give all you can.*" Community was defined as internal membership. Only a few miles away, poor communities existed in vastly different financial condi-tions. Community stopped when one left the suburb.

Sadly, my experience with this suburban Houston church was not unique, and if we review the national statistics, it is more the norm. I researched American church budget priorities, and while there are some differences between surveys, those differences are not significant. *Christi-anity Today International* funded a 2009 Church Budget Priorities Survey on operating budgets excluding capital fundraising. Over 1,100 churches responded, and while the survey does not specify the denominational affiliations, they are likely to be United States evangelical churches. On church operating budget expenses, 664 churches responded. Among the results: Salaries and wages comprise the largest expense in church operating budgets at 38 percent. A distant second is building at 12 percent. The remaining 50 percent is almost evenly distributed among other expenses, ranging from 3 percent to 8 percent of church operating budgets. Domestic and international mission support totaled 10 percent (average expenses for all churches).[23]

The Evangelical Christian Credit Union (ECCU) surveyed its Ministry Advisory Panel related to 2013 budget allocations. Personnel expenses averaged 58 percent, facilities 18 percent, and evangelism/outreach/benevolences totaled 6 percent. Benevolences are funds that churches spend on helping communities or give to other nonprofits that help communities. The ECCU survey references and compares its data with the 2009 CTI survey, but does not specify the statistics on the churches surveyed or why they differ.[24]

In 1982, Joe Walker published a book, *Money in the Church*, on United Methodist finances. He wrote, "Year after year, the church gave 15 percent of its total money to benevolences" and in 1979, "only 14 percent went to benevolences."[25] A later publication, *Money Matters: Personal Giving in American Churches*, did a broader 1996 survey that concluded: "The proportion of total expenditures going to mission work and programs is quite uniform across denominations, ranging from 10.7 percent (Catholics) to 15.7 percent (Baptists)."[26] With Christian denomination membership declining, it seems reasonable that external giving has declined over time as fewer members mean less money that can be allocated to variable cost items like mission outreach. Expenses for personnel and facilities get allocated over fewer members. My experiences with Protestant denominational churches are consistent with these surveys. If one gives 10 percent of their household income to their church, and the church gives 10 percent to external missions, then one gives only 1 percent of their money to others. Almost all resources go internally. *"Give all you can"* does not mean "give all you can to yourself."

---

23. "Church Budget Priorities Survey," 8.

24. "2013 Church Budget Allocations," 2.

25. Walker, *Money in the Church*, 25.

26. Hage et al., *Money Matters*, 34.

I am certainly not against church funds being used internally. Having a church building, staff, and associated costs provide for the Christian community, which is needed. Community worship, prayer, discipleship, and service are central to the Christian faith. But there must be a balance. Bottom line: church finances are too heavily focused inwardly. Urban activist and author, Robert Lupton, agrees:

> The local church is an institution with institutional needs. It is important to understand this. It begins with an informal group of like-minded people who come together for fellowship and worship, it evolves into a structured organization with budgets and staff and buildings, and finally it matures into an enduring institution. It functions like all other institutions—with a stated mission and an intrinsic motivation to preserve and protect its own interests. The lion's share of church budgets are spent on meeting the needs of the congregation, not for the needs of outside communities.[27]

It is possible to balance internal and external financial resources, but it takes a committed, long-term missional strategy (more about this in the *Be Missional* step). For example, Memorial Drive Presbyterian Church (MDPC) in Houston started in 1954 with 75 members in an affluent area, but began with different priorities. Here is a statement from the MDPC website:

> We are committed to a Dollar-for-Dollar benevolence program. Since the church's inception in 1954 and continuing to the present, we annually set a goal of matching the money spent in the operation of the church and its programs with giving to those in need in the community and the world. Annually, this works out to approximately $4 million that goes directly to missionaries, mission agencies, and mission partners, both here in Houston and globally. The allocation and administration of these funds is the responsibility of MDPC's Outreach Ministries, who annually review funding requests, visit partners, and provide emotional and physical support to the 140+ beneficiaries of this congregation's commitment to generosity.[28]

MDPC's membership has grown from fewer than 100 members into a very large church. Balancing internal needs with serving the external community does not inhibit growth. My belief is that MDPC's founding financial strategy was one of the reasons for its successful membership growth.

27. Lupton, *Toxic Charity*, 70.
28. Memorial Drive Presbyterian Church, "Our Story," paras. 1–2.

So how do Christians know if their churches or nonprofits are fiscally responsible and get the right balance between internal and external funding? It starts with reviewing financial statements and checking the allocation of expenses between internal and external. Make sure you ask questions if the split is not clear. For example, there may be internal staff that spend time and resources on external projects. Make a list of external projects and determine their allocations. Church contributions to unaffiliated nonprofits may have internal costs within the nonprofits and these must be allocated. A good metric is a maximum 20 percent for internal expenses. When doing missional work, divide the costs between the sender and receiver. Both benefit, but those who are receiving should acquire at least 50 percent of the total missional budget. There are so many opportunities to invest our resources, which is wonderful, but one must decide prudently.

Wesley's theology of providence covers personal, workplace, and church resources. It is an all-inclusive theology. Working Christians are responsible for prudently, efficiently, and effectively being good stewards of God's providence. Through prayer, reading Scripture, and listening to the Holy Spirit, we make decisions on how best to manage God's providence. Providence management begins with our personal resources and extends into the workplace, church, and other organizations. Managing God's providence relates to achieving self-actualization, caring for the community (Christian and beyond) and taking steps toward the new creation. After we *Honor*, *Master*, and *Manage*, we must next *Exhibit Christlike Character*.

Step 4: Exhibit Christlike Character

> *Let your fellow workers see the light*
> *of Christ within you.*
> *Our character is founded upon humility,*
> *gratitude and courage.*

I think we might find more non-Christians turning to Christ if we as Christians concentrated considerably more on a God-honoring lifestyle than simply on evangelistic strategies. Obviously we need both. But I think we are shooting ourselves in the foot if we try to witness apart from Christlike conduct.[1]

—DOUG SHERMAN AND WILLIAM HENDRICKS,
AUTHORS OF YOUR WORK MATTERS TO GOD

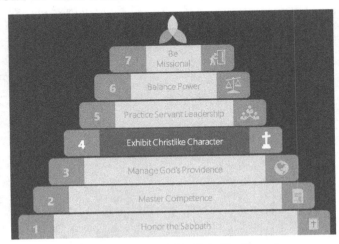

Figure 19—Step 4: Exhibit Christlike Character

1. Sherman and Hendricks, *Your Work Matters to God*, 70.

MY FIRST TRADING JOB in Houston was in Shell's products trading group. I was the junior gasoline trader working with Randy, the senior gasoline trader. Randy was a very competent trader who knew the refined products markets, the external professional traders, and how to add value to Shell. He kindly mentored me, and I owe my later trading successes to him because I learned from one of the best in the business. He was also an ethical and community-minded Christian.

Randy and I both worked for Larry, an older gentleman who was streetwise and tough. Larry understood the trading business, both technically and culturally. Larry had returned to Shell after taking a leave of absence for health reasons. At a fairly late age, Larry developed a deadly form of leukemia and underwent massive chemotherapy. He was very sick and almost died during the treatments. Thankfully, he recovered and was free of cancer for the remainder of his life.

Larry was a dedicated career employee. His Shell friends visited him in the hospital and sent their heartfelt wishes for his full recovery. For reasons unexplained, Larry was worried about losing his job and feared that, even if he recovered, his trading managerial career was over. This added stress on top of his illness. Steve, who was head of Shell's refining business at that time, heard of Larry's illness and stress.

Steve was a soft-spoken Christian who attended my church in Houston. He quietly served on the Session, chaired several church committees, and cared deeply for his family. Steve called Larry while he was in the hospital and told him that his job in products trading would be waiting for him after his recovery. This reassurance calmed Larry and helped him concentrate on getting healthy. Steve exhibited Christlike character. He took the time to help someone in need when he could have easily delegated it to another manager under him or let the Human Resources department make the company policy decisions. He did it quietly, without fanfare or self-promotion. Steve's actions came from his Christian beliefs, something I had witnessed in him at our church.

After an extended absence, Larry returned as Shell's products trading manager just as Steve had promised. I heard about Steve's kindness from Larry when I was trading in his group. Larry was always thankful to Steve and proud to work for Shell because of people like Steve who exhibited the light of Christ in the world.

Character comes from the Greek word *charaktēr*, which translates as a "graving tool." Theologically, moral character is one of the traits forming a person's personality that gives insight into their moral qualities. Being a character is not the same as *having* character. One can stand out by being witty, loud, talented, or charismatic, yet not have character. Character is part of your being.

If a Christian declares their faith in Christ but does not exhibit Christlike character, then the community does not witness Christ in that person. Moltmann writes that "Christ is the foundation for salvation and new life. And for that reason christology and Christian ethics cannot be separated."[2] Virtues matter in Christian work because our skills can be used for or against community and for or against progress toward the new creation. Dr. Larive, an Episcopal Priest, strongly believes that "virtues are necessary, that is, ingrained dispositions to behave temperately, honestly, justly, and so forth."[3]

Scripture is filled with writings on morality, ethics, and character. These are God-revealed morals that instill character. In the Old Testament, God gave Moses the Ten Commandments (Exod 20:7–17, Deut 5:11–21) and Hebrew laws. In the New Testament, Jesus preached the Sermon on the Mount (Matt 5:1—7:27), and Paul writes of the fruit of the Spirit (Gal 5:22–26). My seminary required all students to take a course on Christian ethics because it is so central to our being as Christians. We are called to exhibit Christlike character 24/7.[4]

Character is both a journey and a destination. We build character daily through the journey of life. Character is molded by our parents, family, friends, churches, schools, work, and institutions. We get conflicting messages about character and must make choices. We make mistakes and learn from them. But as Christians, we should strive to exhibit Christlike character. It is our ultimate destination to be fully obedient to Christ.

Character is learned through community. Our first community is our family, led by our parents or other adults. If the family unit is Christian, this is usually the first instance to learn about Christlike character. If we were raised in the church, then we learn about Christlike character from our church worship, teachers, and service experiences. We read Scripture, and the Spirit moves within us to shape our Christlike character. The revealed word instructs, molds, and moves our very being. As Moltmann writes,

2. Moltmann, *Way of Jesus Christ*, 42.

3. Larive, *After Sunday*, 163.

4. Costa, *God at Work*, 26.

"To know Jesus does not simply mean learning the facts of christological dogma. It means learning to know him in the praxis of discipleship."[5]

Our Christlike character is founded upon humility, gratitude, and courage. These virtues must be practiced during our work. David Brooks, author of *The Road to Character*, writes:

> We don't live for happiness, we live for holiness . . . All human beings seek to lead lives not just of pleasure, but of purpose, righteousness, and virtue . . . Life is essentially a moral drama, not a hedonistic one.[6]

And although this book is about work, Christlike character and obedience to God have priority over work. We must be careful not to turn work into an idol. Work must be balanced with other aspects of life such as family, friends, and leisure. We must not become addicted to work.[7]

Humility

I went to high school in a small south Texas town outside of Corpus Christi. As there were only about 200 in my graduating class, I knew most of my fellow classmates. I was in the group of students taking the upper-level classes, and we attended many classes together. These students became my closest high school friends.

One particular outstanding student was Mike, the son of the First Baptist Church's senior pastor. First Baptist was the largest, most influential church in my small town. Mike's mother taught senior English and was an excellent teacher. You might think that Mike had two strikes against him—he was a preacher's kid with a mother who taught in his high school (I had one strike against me since *my* mother taught English!). Yet, Mike was always . . . Mike. He was naturally courteous, with a broad smile. He sang so well that he made All-State choir. He was popular and was elected to Student Council and became our Senior Class President. Mike was also very active in his father's church. When there were high school dances, First Baptist offered alternative church activities because they disapproved of dancing. The only time I saw Mike at a school dance was when he presented

---

5. Moltmann, *Way of Jesus Christ*, 43.

6. Brooks, *Road to Character*, 262.

7. Keller, *Every Good Endeavor*, 27.

an award at prom, since this was a duty of the senior class president. Mike dressed up, presented the award, and then promptly departed.

In my freshman English class, we read one of Shakespeare's plays aloud. When Mike was called on, he read his portion of the play, but he skipped any words or phrases with sexual connotations. As a teenager, this shocked me—what teenage boy would not want to say something sexual in high school with the teacher's approval?

Mike was quiet by high school standards. I never heard him belittle anyone, swear, or get angry. He just smiled, joked with his fellow students, and blended in. Teenagers can be cruel to others who don't play the popularity games, yet nobody mocked Mike for his beliefs, values, or choices. In fact, we all loved Mike because he was so centered. Mike knew who he was, and he was not going to change his character to be popular with the "in crowd." As I said, Mike was always Mike.

At the end of my senior year, we assembled in the auditorium for senior awards. The last awards were the class valedictorian and salutatorian. It had been a close contest over my four years of high school. Mike was an excellent student and strived to obtain top grades. But another student, John, took valedictorian honors; Mike was the salutatorian. What happened next remained with me for the rest of my life. Mike walked across the auditorium stage to John and shook his hand. Mike told him that it was a good, fair competition and John was the top scholar. Mike thanked John for making him a better student and wished John well in his university studies. I sat there in awe of Mike's Christlike humility—no bitterness or sadness displayed, only love. Humility is the foundational platform of Christlike character.

For all the years I worked in energy trading, I found that humility was rarely a virtue exhibited on the trading floor. Traders who performed a good trade that added value to the trade books made sure that the deal and who made it were well publicized. Good news traveled fast and always seemed to reach the highest management levels at record speed. Just as modern athletes openly celebrate their winning plays, traders celebrate, boasting of their deeds. The opposite was true with trading losses; silence reigned, and after the daily trade book settled, I (in my managerial role) was informed of the loss because it would be posted by the time I arrived in the office the next day. I had to explain the loss to my manager since the traders did not want to openly claim it to senior management.

When the year-end trading bonuses were debated, humility and community were rarely present. When asked if a trading team's financial results were improved through the support of another trading team, the answer was usually "yes, and we need this trading team." When asked how much of their financial results should be shared with the other trading teams who supported them, the answer was "none" or "it can't be quantified." Humility requires the truth even when others get the rewards.

Several years after I started trading in Houston, a trading manager retired. He called me and said that I had surprised trading management. When I asked him why, he said that the trading managers thought I would fail as a trader since I was soft-spoken and less aggressive. I wasn't "trading material." His words shocked me, as I thought that trading was a competency, not an egotistical competition. It is possible to prosper with humility in the rough-and-tumble environment of the financial markets.

Humility is accepting the fact that you don't know everything. When humans are compared to God, there *is* no comparison. Humility is recognizing our own weaknesses and sinfulness. Humility is reading the Gospels and understanding that grace was given through the humble character of Jesus Christ, as Scripture tells us:

> Let the same mind be in you that was in Christ Jesus, who, though he was in the form of God, did not regard equality with God as something to be exploited, but emptied himself, taking the form of a slave, being born in human likeness. And being found in human form, he *humbled* [my emphasis] himself and became obedient to the point of death—even death on a cross. Therefore God also highly exalted him and gave him the name that is above every name, so that at the name of Jesus every knee should bend, in heaven and on earth and under the earth, and every tongue should confess that Jesus Christ is Lord, to the glory of God the Father. (Phil 2:5–11)

Humility allows for doubt, openness, and empathy. It gives you the space to listen to others without judgment, even when you vehemently disagree with their words or actions. Peter M. Senge, author of *The Fifth Discipline* and a renowned business strategist, wrote:

> Without uncertainty or doubt, there is no foundation for tolerance. If there is one "right view," which we will generally see as our own, we have no space for the possibility that a different point of view may be valid. Because of that, we have no empathy for

those with different views. Because of that, of course, we have no humility.[8]

It is difficult and most likely impossible to see and understand the world when we are puffed up with ego. Our inflated attitude covers the eyes and ears, shutting out the surrounding world, since ego turns us inward. Humility allows the eyes and ears to focus on the world around us and opens us up to questions. Humility allows us to see ourselves as broken, living in a broken world. "As [Saint] Augustine put it, "Where there's humility, there's majesty; where there's weakness, there's might . . ."[9]

As I reflect on my life, I see so many instances where I failed to exhibit humility. I displayed my framed university degrees and honors for all to see instead of having the inner confidence of the knowledge I gained through education. I touted my trading profits and successes rather than realizing that my successes were part of a team effort. I discussed my running times rather than appreciating the improved physical fitness achieved through the difficult workouts. I spent time recounting my life to others when I should have listened more empathetically to their life experiences. I worried and stressed about going up the corporate ladder instead of concentrating on improving my competency or growing in faith. Life is a journey, and I still have much work to do in humbly following Christ. Brooks writes:

> Defeating weakness often means quieting the self. Only by quieting the self, by muting the sound of your own ego, can you see the world clearly. Only by quieting the self can you be open to the external sources of strengths you will need.[10]

Gratitude

Each year in early February, Trading gave bonuses to all eligible employees based on their contribution to the year's performance. This was a blessing to reward good performance as well as a difficult message to employees who did not perform against their agreed targets. Bob (not his real name) was an experienced and competent employee who worked in my team. He had a long history of good trading results and was highly paid.

8. Greenleaf, *Servant Leadership*, 354.
9. Brooks, *Road to Character*, 205.
10. Brooks, *Road to Character*, 265.

During the previous summer while I was on vacation, a trading position in Bob's trading team declined by tens of millions of dollars in just five days. I read emails from afar during the biggest trading loss of my career. When I called Bob, he gave incomplete answers as to why this was happening. When I returned, Bob did not want to discuss the loss. To learn and hopefully not repeat a negative trading position, we must be open to discussions and dive into the details. My analytics team and I spent a week dissecting the trade book loss. We finally determined that our trading exposures were not being calculated correctly in our IT systems. The trade book had much more risk than what our trading systems calculated, although we were still within our trading authorities.

At Bob's year-end review, we discussed his performance, including the substantial loss. His group was able to make up most of the loss by the end of the year, and they achieved their performance targets. It would have been an exceptional year except for that large mid-year loss. I told Bob that he had not taken accountability for the loss and that I'd had to perform all the investigative work. I detailed Bob's professional shortcomings in the personnel system, and Bob signed off on my report.

On bonus day, I called Bob into my office and handed him his bonus. It was less than in previous years. He looked at his bonus and started swearing. He unloaded his personal feelings about his lower-than-expected bonus and told me how unfairly he felt he had been treated.

I listened until I'd heard enough. I stood up, and Bob sat down. I reminded him about our year-end performance discussions and recounted all the years when he had been rewarded. I then spoke to Bob about gratitude, as his compensation was very generous—that he should be grateful for receiving such providence even when the amount didn't match his expectations. Most of the trading floor would quickly exchange their bonuses for Bob's. I finally asked him to go home, reflect about gratitude, and think some more about his comments, especially in light of our previous performance discussions. Bob was quiet, and then left my office.

This meeting shook me deeply. Bob was a Christian who was blessed with a lovely family and good health. He regularly attended church and was normally a respectful, responsible person. His lack of gratitude shocked me, given his committed Christian faith. This encounter showed me how money and entitlement can potentially warp our character. As Dr. Fox says,

"Authentic work comes from a deep place of gratitude. Indeed, work is about gratitude; it is the expression of our gratitude for being here."[11]

Gratitude supports humility. The two cannot be separated. "Thankfulness," the Archbishop of Canterbury, Michael Ramsey, said, "is a soil in which pride does not easily grow."[12]

Most days, I rise early to read from a short devotional book and pray. I always give thanks to God for my health, family, friends, and providence. I reflect on the previous day with gratitude, even when it wasn't a good day. Gratitude centers my character, so when life's journey turns downward, I balance it with gratitude for God's many gifts. My relationships improve when I give thanks, as I don't take my friends, family, and community for granted. My hope for the new creation increases when I reflect on the Holy Spirit at work in the world today.

My favorite holiday is Thanksgiving. I love the smells of roast turkey, sweet potatoes, and pumpkin pie. My favorite part of Thanksgiving is giving thanks. Sometimes, before blessing the food, we ask each person to name something they're thankful for. For me, it is hard to pare down my list to only one thing.

Christians also unite around another meal: the Lord's Supper. When Jesus celebrated the Passover the night before he died, he first gave thanks: "Then he took a cup, and after giving thanks . . . he took a loaf of bread, and when he had given thanks . . ." (Luke 22:17–19).

Gratitude comes from the Latin *gratitudo*, meaning an expression of praise and devotion. Christians come forward to receive God's grace during the Lord's Supper. We do this with *open hands* because we can't receive God's grace with clenched fists. Open hands symbolize our need for grace and our gratitude to Jesus Christ, the giver of this gift. "Thanks be to God for his indescribable gift" (2 Cor 9:15)!

Work is a blessing that enables self-actualization, serves the community, and moves our world closer to the new creation. We work at exhibiting gratitude. Even our darkest days can be brighter when we reflect upon God's blessings. The surrounding community will feel our gratitude, and hopefully will develop the same virtue of gratitude.

11. Fox, *Reinvention of Work*, 126.
12. Brooks, *Road to Character*, 8.

Courage

In January 2003, I was wrapping up a yearlong trading integration project. My supervisor, Mark, called me into his office and asked me to attend several days of review meetings on a large IT project. I knew that the project had problems, but after a few hours of listening to the project audit team describe the issues, it seemed that the word "disaster" described it better. The project team had spent its authorized budget without delivering the agreed-upon requirements. Poor project management and soured relationships between the traders and IT were the major problems. The IT manager over the project had resigned.

Mark called me into his office and asked me what I'd heard during the meetings. I described the problems and said, "It's a mess." Mark then told me that Trading management had decided that I should take over the project leadership.

For the next month, I restructured the project's 100 business and IT employees into five separate, more manageable project units. My team put together a project budget for senior management approval. Mark requested that I seek approval for the budget at a senior trading management meeting in London. I flew to London for the meeting and saw that two managing directors, the most senior executives, were there. One of them was Paul who was highly competent in trading.

I started my presentation with the bad news first: the history of the IT project and its failures. I wanted to get this out of the way and then concentrate on the project's future. In the middle of explaining the project's failures, Paul yelled, "Stop!" He angrily asked, "Who managed this project?"

I replied, "The IT vice president, and he has left the company."

Paul asked, "And who was his boss?"

This put me in a terrible position as Mark, my supervisor, was his manager. Naming Mark would indict my boss. I looked at Paul, not knowing what to say.

Then Mark spoke. "Paul, I managed him."

Paul glared at Mark, and the room went absolutely quiet. Peter, the financial vice president, said, "Paul, we were all deceived. We all take responsibility for the project's failures."

Paul, who knew and trusted Peter, calmed down and asked me to continue. I next presented the new plans to complete the project and requested additional funding. Paul listened carefully, asked good questions, and finally said, "I like it. You have my approval. Don't let me down."

I left the room exhausted from the stress. Mark later congratulated me for my courage in front of the top Trading executives. However, I was not the courageous person. Mark acknowledged his accountability—*he* was courageous. But the most courageous person was Peter, who could have stayed quiet. Mark could have taken all of Paul's anger and perhaps punishment. It was Peter who understood community and acknowledged his related responsibility for the poor outcome. Peter's courage showed his true character of honesty within community, possibly to his own detriment. He showed courageous character.

Most people connect courage with the battlefield or facing death from defending a conviction. But courage happens each day—with humility and gratitude. It is shown daily in our workplace character. Courage is speaking with integrity and saying no to dishonest practices; treating all with respect when others are disrespectful; evaluating employees professionally and fairly even though they have higher-level management friends who may disagree with your assessment. Courage is presenting all relevant facts even if they may cause a project to be dropped and disrupt your career. It's seeking diverse opinions rather than surrounding yourself with yes people. Courage is telling your boss that you respectfully disagree with a decision on a major issue, or resigning from an unethical company.

Courage is displayed through disciplined practice learned over a lifetime. It actually gets easier to be courageous when it's practiced daily because those around you don't test you as often; they know your character and how you will react to unethical practices. I once gave a presentation to a group of Shell employees on how to succeed in trading. My wife was at the meeting, and the person next to her asked later, "Your husband is a Christian, right? I feel quite sure by the way he spoke." If your fellow employees recognize your Christlike character, it might lower the potential for questionable activities or unethical practices.

Courage allows a Christian to be humble. Humility does not denote a weak person. Humility paired with courage is a powerful position that allows Christians to stand tall in the face of stiff opposition. Courage is taking a stand with Christ against evil in the workplace. By going into the workplace with Christlike courage, Christians can change the workplace for the better; the marketplace is not a neutral environment. People come to work with their beliefs, prejudices, and values within them.[13] It is a Christian's job to be a force for good in a broken world. Christians need to

13. Sherman and Hendricks, *Your Work Matters to God*, 241.

display Christlike courage in the workplace. Every Christian must choose their character daily, and Christ is the ultimate example. When we *Exhibit Christlike Character*, we become a contrast community. Jago Wynne, Associate Rector at Holy Trinity Clapham (United Kingdom) and author of *Working Without Wilting*, makes this very point:

> While others might be hungering and thirsting for more money, more status, or more sexual fulfillment, we'll be thirsting for righteousness. We'll be people who say, "I'm sorry." We'll be people who say, "I forgive you." We'll be people who know we make mistakes, so admit them, and are understanding when others make mistakes as well. We'll be utterly sincere and totally transparent in our dealings with people. We'll be authentic—our actions will match our thoughts; our character on a Sunday will match our character on a Monday. We'll long for peace for our colleagues—horizontally between them when there are tensions, and vertically when there is tension between them and God. We will want peace and we will actually look to make it happen.[14]

To "make it happen," we will need to *Practice Servant Leadership*.

---

14. Wynne, *Working Without Wilting*, 99.

Step 5: Practice Servant Leadership

> *The great leader is seen as servant first.*
> *Our leadership skills come from God*
> *and are used to develop people and*
> *serve the community.*

It has generally been my experience that the very top people of truly great organizations are servant-leaders. They are the most humble, the most reverent, the most open, the most teachable, the most respectful, the most caring, and the most determined. When people with the formal authority or positional power refuse to use that authority and power except as a last resort, their moral authority increases because it is obvious that they have subordinated their ego and positional power and use reasoning, persuasion, kindness, empathy, and, in short, *trustworthiness* instead.[1]

—ROBERT K. GREENLEAF, FOUNDER OF
THE GREENLEAF CENTER FOR SERVANT LEADERSHIP

1. Greenleaf, *Servant Leadership*, 12 (emphasis his).

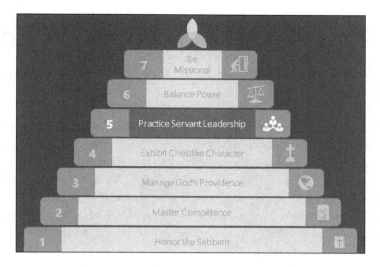

Figure 20—Step 5: Practice Servant Leadership

IN 2006, I RETURNED to Houston from The Netherlands and started a new assignment. I managed the North Region's gas and power trading, marketing, and business development activities. This was my first managerial position supervising multiple offices stretching from Vancouver to Houston. My first action was to visit the various offices and meet the employees. I scheduled dinners where we could socialize. The employees were listening and watching me as much as I was carefully learning about their business.

One of the North Region's offices was in Syracuse. The office then had about twenty-five employees. Almost all employees had long-term ties to the Syracuse area; they were a tight community. I grew to love the city of Syracuse and these dedicated employees. While the Syracuse winters were cold and snowy, the trading employees were warm and hospitable.

After my introductory office visits, my boss, Mark, asked me about my initial impressions of the North Region. I went through the various offices, their business potential, and the people. When I came to the Syracuse office, I asked, "Why do we trade power from Syracuse?" Shell's global trading was at that time centralized in major trading hubs: Houston, Calgary, London, Moscow, and Singapore. This was done for strict trading controls and to minimize back-office support costs. Syracuse was not a major trading hub.

Mark smiled and said, "I was hoping you'd question the need for a Syracuse power trading office. It has grown over time, and the Syracuse office continues to demand more back-office support. We need to decide whether to grow the power trading business in Syracuse or move it to Houston."

I recruited a financial analyst to help me develop the pros and cons of moving the Syracuse power trading business to Houston. The move would reduce expenses, tighten trading controls, and better develop the relocated employees in the Houston trading hub. There was a downside—we estimated that 40 percent of the Syracuse employees would not transfer to Houston for various reasons. I presented my analysis to Mark and his leadership team. I received approval for all transferred positions to go to existing Syracuse employees. We could have hired several new positions in Houston and saved moving expenses, but we valued the existing employees and did not want to lose the skills of the Syracuse employees. I wanted Syracuse power trading to continue working as a team. All would have jobs if they moved to Houston.

On a cold February day, I flew to Syracuse and met over dinner with the three office managers. I informed them of the decision to move power trading to Houston, and told them I'd make the announcement public the next day. The two local Syracuse managers had not seen this announcement coming. I explained the rationale and that all affected employees would have positions in Houston.

The next day, I gathered the Syracuse office together, along with Human Resources personnel. I went through the decision, the rationale, and the way forward. The employees were quiet and in shock. When I was done, Stan, a power trader, said, "Ken, we are all family here. You've broken up our family." This summed up their feelings. I spoke personally to anyone who wanted to speak with me. Later that evening, I returned to Houston.

After about a week, I received a phone call from the Human Resources employee assigned to the Syracuse move, who said that the office was fighting it, and they needed me back in Syracuse. I told my boss, Mark, that the office was resisting the move, and that I was flying back to Syracuse to address their issues. He said, "Then Syracuse will hear the news directly from me. I'll go with you." He changed his busy schedule, and we quickly caught a plane to Syracuse.

The next morning, we called a meeting for all employees. Mark went through the rationale for the move and the process for making the decision, and he concluded with, "The decision is final." To questions and pleas, Mark stood firm and said, "We've made this decision. You must make yours. We desire that all affected employees move to Houston. It's a good city for your families. I moved there with my family. Your career potential will be better in this larger office, and you'll have more professional growth opportunities. We will work to make this transition as smooth as possible for you and your families."

After this meeting, the Syracuse employees made their individual decisions. Miraculously, only one Syracuse employee decided not to move to Houston. Over time, the Syracuse employees found Houston to be welcoming and better than their initial expectations. After a year, I presented an analysis of the move to Mark's leadership team and showed the positive benefits both to Trading's financial results and professionally to the employees. The move was a success.

Mark was a servant leader. He allowed me time to investigate the problem and develop a solution. He supported my recommendations and empathized when I struggled with balancing company profits and employee needs. When the Syracuse office rebelled, he backed me up. Mark could have distanced himself from confrontations with the Syracuse office and blamed me for any failures. Instead, he took the time to support me in front of the Syracuse office.

Servant Leadership

The founder of the modern servant leadership movement, Robert Greenleaf, stated: "*The great leader is seen as servant first,* and that simple fact is the key to his greatness."[2] Mark developed my leadership skills. I grew under his mentoring. He did not *give* me the answers; he *guided* and *supported* me through my development journey. When others looked only at the company's bottom line, Mark understood the needs of the employees. By keeping the Syracuse family together during the move by offering all affected employees positions in Houston, the company retained the power trading team. Mark understood that community was important to Syracuse.

The servant leader makes his first priority other people. The servant leader's primary responsibility is the growth of those he serves.[3] Do the served self-actualize? Do they become the persons that God created in God's image? How can I assist the served to become future servant leaders?

---

2. Greenleaf, *Servant Leadership*, 21 (emphasis his).

3. Greenleaf, *Servant Leadership*, 27.

Jesus was a servant leader. He was a rabbi, a teacher, to his disciples. When James and John, his disciples, wanted places of prominence beside him, Jesus used it as a teachable moment:

> So Jesus called them and said to them, "You know that among the Gentiles those whom they recognize as their rulers lord it over them, and their great ones are tyrants over them. But it is not so among you; but whoever wishes to become great among you must be your servant, and whoever wishes to be first among you must be slave of all. For the Son of Man came not to be served but to serve, and to give his life a ransom for many." (Mark 10:42–45)

Even at the Last Supper, the disciples did not understand servant leadership. They debated who of the twelve was considered the greatest! Jesus needed another reminder for the disciples to understand servant leadership:

> But he said to them, "The kings of the Gentiles lord it over them; and those in authority over them are called benefactors. But not so with you; rather the greatest among you must become like the youngest, and the leader like one who serves. For who is greater, the one who is at the table or the one who serves? Is it not the one at the table? But I am among you as one who serves." (Luke 22:25–27)

Servant leadership is not assuming leadership for personal power, but taking the leadership role to serve. Those in leadership positions are usually paid more than those they supervise; however, taking a leadership role for material gain will most likely result in personal discontent and regret. Instead, we should use competency and leadership skills to serve our organization, our supervised employees, our customers, and our communities. The extra money is just icing on the cake. "The servant-leader *is* servant first."[4] Leaders that strive for personal power and wealth are not servant-leaders.

The theological model of work starts with self-actualization. Leadership gifts come from God and are used to develop people so that they can self-actualize. Leaders are in the business of growing people. The process is bidirectional—the served develop their leaders. The result is synergistic. All become more competent, confident, and committed workers.[5]

Self-actualization is balanced with community. Leaders serve the community. Our society tends to see leaders as individuals with special

4. Greenleaf, *Servant Leadership*, 27 (emphasis his).
5. Greenleaf, *Servant Leadership*, 159.

leadership competencies. However, the complexities in our modern society require teamwork and coordination by many workers.[6] Leadership without community is not leadership.

As Christian leaders, we work to move our community toward the promised new creation. Greenleaf saw this same vision: Leadership is "the capacity of a human community to shape its future."[7] Jesus started with only a few disciples in his ancient world ruled by the Roman military. He trained a small team of committed followers in servant leadership. After a little more than 300 years, the Roman state became a Christian community. One individual using servant leadership can change the world.

Disrespectful Leadership

Trading leadership held regularly scheduled review meetings. One manager, Rick (not his real name), went to the extreme on scheduling leadership meetings. He held monthly leadership meetings and four quarterly reviews each year. These all-day grueling meetings were filled with performance reviews, business presentations, and intense debates. Individuals or groups presented on topics or requested approval for a major business deal. For the quarterly reviews, a detailed analysis of the recently published results was distributed in advance and painstakingly reviewed for hours. No managers could hide from bad results. Good results were scrutinized for ways to add more value.

Before transferring into Rick's leadership team, I normally enjoyed these leadership meetings. Besides having fewer of them, my earlier leadership teams were more collegial. There were tough discussions, but we respected one another and debated the business, not the person. This was not the case with Rick. His leadership style was to shame people with the hope of forcing them to improve. Nobody wanted to be the victim of Rick's public shaming experiences. Rick would promptly arrive at the leadership meetings and sit upright in his chair with his review book squarely on the table. I learned not to look directly at him for fear that I would receive his first wrath. My hope was that he would be in a pleasant mood; I was usually disappointed. The room quieted when he entered. His first words usually included no greetings, but were a frontal assault on someone in the room.

6. Greenleaf, *Servant Leadership*, 359.

7. Greenleaf, *Servant Leadership*, 358.

The quarterly review financial package was prepared by our analyst, a professional who scrambled to assemble the financial information in time for the review. I knew the difficulty of preparing the information, and I helped him by reviewing the materials before the leadership meeting. I had been on Rick's leadership team for less than six months when Rick walked into a quarterly review meeting and spent the first fifteen minutes shaming our analyst's work. He listed the pages that had typos or unclear wording. He said that he disliked the format even though the analyst's job was to assemble the information, not develop it. I felt sorry for the analyst who was the victim of Rick's tirade. He quietly accepted the verbal barrage and walked out with his head down.

I saw this shaming time and time again against other professionals during my years in this assignment. I had to counsel my team on how to present to Rick. I coached them to never get upset at Rick and just calmly answer his questions. Those who pushed back during the shaming sessions incurred additional anger and negativity. During our one-to-one meetings, I tried to carefully discuss his leadership style, but I was unsuccessful in upwardly managing him. An executive coach was hired for him, and this helped for a few months, but Rick eventually reverted to his disrespectful leadership style. Twice, after being coached by Human Resources, he apologized to me behind closed doors. Rick knew the difference between right and wrong. He just chose not to be a servant-leader. He had a brilliant mind, and we rarely disagreed on business matters. Our disagreements were on leadership style. Rick told me that I wasn't hard enough on my team. I told him that I asked hard questions during meetings, and then addressed the personal issues and tough coaching behind closed doors rather than in public. I wanted to uplift employees. Rick wanted to tear them down and exert his authoritative power over them. Rick's leadership style was based on power and material gain. He controlled their careers and wanted all to know who was in charge.

Rick had many other ways to show people his power. Our leadership team regularly traveled around to the regional offices. Cars would transport the leadership team from the airport to the office, and Rick would always wait until all bags were loaded before placing his bag on top of ours. Then, he would carefully remove his coat and place it neatly on his bag—over our bags and coats—so it wouldn't be wrinkled.

After a long day of meetings and dinner, he gathered us together for drinks. Many of the discussions he led were about other employees. Sadly, he spoke negatively about his peers and the more senior managers. I usually sat in silence, hoping to end the long day as quickly as possible. I rarely heard anything positive about others from Rick except for a few individuals who worked for him.

Reviewing work products and addressing employee issues is part of a leader's job description. "But one cannot *lead* from a predominantly negative posture."[8] Having worked under Rick, I witnessed that affirmation leadership is much more effective than negative leadership. Rick should have shown love to others, not because they performed in ways he approved or jumped when he said "jump," but because they were also made, like him, in God's image. Giving love and showing respect to others is what servant leadership embodies, as former CEO of Applied Energy Services Dennis Bakke writes:

> It is love that allows us to give up our power to control. It is love that allows us to treat each person in our organization with respect and dignity. Love sends people around the world to serve others. Love inspires people to work with greater purpose.[9]

Apologizing When You are Wrong

During an IT project, I worked with a great team of highly competent employees. Connie was a skilled process professional whose role was to track, analyze, and document system processes. This allowed IT to improve speed and efficiency. During one meeting, someone suggested that I review some trading processes because of my trading experience. Connie said, "Ken hasn't done trading for over a year. I doubt he can do this review."

I took her statement personally and uncharacteristically blasted her: "How do you know what I can and cannot do? You're not a trader, and I certainly know trading processes." The room got quiet, as I was the most senior person in the room. Connie quietly said, "Fine."

I went back to my room still angry from Connie's comment. Upon reflection, I had disrespected Connie, a very competent, hard-working, and dedicated person. I asked another person who was at the meeting for her reflections. The feedback was that Connie had a right to express her opinion, and my statement may have shut down others from raising their concerns during future meetings.

8. Greenleaf, *Servant Leadership*, 248 (emphasis his).
9. Bakke, *Joy at Work*, 241.

I knew that I was wrong and needed to admit it. I wrote a note to Connie apologizing and asking for forgiveness. We later discussed it, and she forgave me. Over the next few years, she worked in my leadership team on other projects, and I was fortunate that my error didn't hurt our future relationship. Connie's forgiveness was genuine. After a number of years, I realized that I should have apologized publicly to Connie in front of the employees who witnessed my outburst. This would have allowed others to witness servant leadership and know that it was acceptable to state an opinion even if a senior person disagreed. Servant leadership is seeking diverse opinions and then listening, even when individuals suggest ideas that you oppose. This is where I failed as a leader with Connie. I should have first listened, then calmly discussed the subject without making it personal.

Servant leadership is respecting all religions, genders, cultures, and other differences that divide humanity. Jesus embraced diversity and went against the norms of the day to dine with sinners, speak to outcasts, and listen to different opinions. Leaders who serve follow Christ's example of respect, dignity, and justice for all. Douglas Hicks, professor of Religion at Colgate University, says:

> The most important task that leaders can perform is to help shape that culture in positive ways . . . They can send clear signals to their employees that religious and other forms of diversity are valued in the company.[10]

Christians *Practice Servant Leadership* because they read the gospel and know that the master servant leader was Jesus Christ. Servant leaders have power over employees, money, and communities, but also know that they are to be obedient to God by serving their community and furthering the new creation.

Leaders must learn to *Balance Power* to subdue their human egos.

---

10. Hicks, *Religion and the Workplace*, 185.

Step 6: Balance Power

> *Power is a double-edged sword—both good and corrupt. Power is used for justice, to save lives, to serve the public's interest, and to move the community toward the new creation.*

Power is actualized only where word and deed have not parted company, where words are not empty and deeds not brutal, where words are not used to violate and destroy but to establish relations and create new realities.[1]

—PROFESSOR JÜRGEN HABERMAS, CHAIR OF PHILOSOPHY
AND SOCIOLOGY AT GOETHE UNIVERSITY

---

1. See Jürgen Habermas, in Lukes, *Power*, 79.

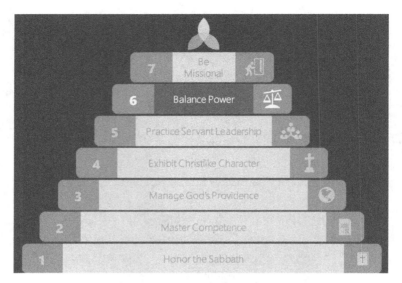

Figure 21—Step 6: Balance Power

MY EARLY CHILDHOOD MEMORIES are fuzzy, but I do remember two major events: the assassination of President John F. Kennedy and the 1964 presidential election. I recall watching Kennedy's burial at Arlington National Cemetery and hearing the twenty-one-gun salute. I did not understand why guns were being fired, but the ceremony was permanently etched into my memory. My other memory was taking sides during first-grade recess on the 1964 presidential election. I was one of the few children advocating Goldwater, and I wondered why so many of my classmates were for Lyndon Johnson. My childhood political views probably reflected those of my parents, or I just liked the name "Goldwater." I certainly did not have any political knowledge at that young age, but I did know that Lyndon Baines Johnson—"LBJ" to most Texans—was the most powerful person in Texas politics and eventually would become the most powerful person in American politics.

LBJ

This book is not about politics, so I won't include my opinions of LBJ. But the overall consensus is that he understood power—how to obtain, retain, and employ it. I read the series of books on LBJ by Robert Caro. Caro is a master of political research; he is a writer whose words paint a realistic picture of LBJ and his family living in Texas during the nineteenth and twentieth centuries. Caro was fascinated with power and researched LBJ's rise to, use of, and fall from power. In the fourth book, *The Years of Lyndon Johnson: The Passage of Power*, Caro described an incident that occurred just after President Kennedy was killed in November 1963, when LBJ and his staff were working on his first presidential address to Congress. "Power always *reveals*." Newly sworn-in President Johnson was huddled around the dining table with his advisors late into the evening and early morning hours. They were drafting Johnson's first major address to a joint session of congress. A key issue was civil rights and how much emphasis to give this divisive subject. Johnson sat silently listening to various advisors discuss the risks and the support that he would need from those who opposed civil rights. Then someone told LBJ "to his face that a President shouldn't spend his time and power on lost causes, no matter how worthy those causes might be. 'Well, what the hell's the presidency for?' Lyndon Johnson replied."[2]

Looking back at this historical period, LBJ should have more vigorously supported civil rights before he had the political power to change federal laws. We do know that once he had the power of the presidency, he used it effectively, some might say brutally, to right a great societal wrong. LBJ will go down in history as the American president who was able to pass the first major federal civil rights legislation since Reconstruction. Although we have yet to reach the promised land, civil rights laws have taken America a step closer toward the new creation where all are equal. Human power can be used to improve God's world.

Jeffrey Pfeffer, professor of Organizational Behavior at Stanford Business School, writes: "Power is part of leadership and is necessary to get things done."[3] It is highly likely that everyone will have some power during their lifetime. You could be a parent, teacher, officer of the law, judge, committee chair, supervisor at work, elder, or board member with power. You don't need to be a US president to hold and employ power.

Our language is filled with power terminology, writes Robert Dahl:

> Power terms evidently cover a very broad category of human relations. Considerable effort and ingenuity have gone into schemes for classifying these relations into various types labelled power, influence, authority, persuasion, dissuasion, inducement, coercion,

2. Caro, *Years of Lyndon Johnson*, xiv–xv (emphasis his).
3. Pfeffer, *Power*, 7.

compulsion, force, and so on, all of which we shall subsume under the collective label power terms.[4]

Power, by itself, is not evil. It's like water; we need it to survive, but we can drown if there is too much of it. The Old Testament's central theme is justice, and it instructs how power is to be used by the powerful. Justice is measured by how the powerful treat the most vulnerable of society: orphans, widows, the aged, and the infirmed. Biblical laws emphasize the strong protecting the weak.[5]

Power should be used for justice, to save lives, to serve the public's interest, and to move our community toward the new creation. Individuals without power can influence others; with power, individuals can profoundly change communities for the better. Power is needed to do good and accomplish beneficial goals that otherwise would languish.[6]

Power is a double-edged sword, with one side cutting deep and dark. Unbalanced, power can convince us that we are a god. In an 1887 letter to Anglican Archbishop Mandell Creighton, Lord John Dalberg-Acton, an English Catholic historian and writer, wrote about the dark side of power: "Power tends to corrupt and absolute power corrupts absolutely. Great men are almost always bad men, even when they exercise influence and not authority."[7]

Roosevelt and Taft

Sadly, friends can become enemies when vying for power. An example of this is the relationship between Theodore "Teddy" Roosevelt and William Howard Taft, the twenty-sixth and twenty-seventh US Presidents. They were close personal friends during their professional careers. Taft served as Roosevelt's Secretary of War. When Roosevelt announced that he would not seek another presidential term, he successfully supported Taft to succeed him. But after retiring, Roosevelt came to dislike Taft's more conservative views and eventually publicly attacked him. This led to a power struggle within the Republican Party, and their friendship dissolved. Roosevelt ran against Taft for the Republican Party's 1912 presidential election. When

4. Robert Dahl, in Lukes, *Power*, 40.

5. Greene, *Thank God it's Monday*, 115.

6. Pfeffer, *Power*, 177.

7. Dalberg-Acton, "Letter to Archbishop Mandell Creighton."

he lost the Republican Party's nomination to Taft, Roosevelt formed the independent Bull Moose Party, which split the Republican vote. Woodrow Wilson became our 28th president, something that would not have happened had Republicans united around a single candidate. Both Roosevelt and Taft lost power; neither could use the power of the presidency anymore. It took years after their bitter rivalry for the friendship to begin again, and Roosevelt died a few years later. Historian Doris Kearns Goodwin wrote:

> As Theodore Roosevelt's casket was lowered into the ground, "an isolated figure" stood "quite apart from the others," William Howard Taft, softly crying. "I want to say to you," Taft later told Roosevelt's sister Bamie, "how glad I am that Theodore and I came together after that long painful interval. Had he died in a hostile state of mind toward me, I would have mourned the fact all my life. I loved him always and cherish his memory."[8]

Power can destroy individuals, families, friendships, communities, and nations. Abusive power can lead to broken homes, financial ruin, incarceration, and even war. Humanity still has not learned to balance the good and bad forces of power. During my professional working years, I have witnessed power rivalries that destroy both relationships and economic value. I have witnessed powerful business leaders destroy careers because of their character flaws. Sadly, I have seen good leaders transform into self-serving individuals after gaining powerful positions. All of this could have been prevented.

Using Power to Right Wrongs

I was working as a London Fuel Oil Trader during the mid-1990s. The work culture was much more formal then and we dressed in business suits. Midday, we assembled together on the trading floor to go eat at the corporate lunch room in the basement. One day, as we were gathering for lunch, my supervisor and his manager were telling us a story about a Nigerian ex-patriate fuel oil trader. At one point in the story, the manager started posturing as an African warrior. He pranced around acting his story like he was holding a spear and shield. He was trying to be funny, but I became very uncomfortable as it mocked Africans.

---

8. Goodwin, *Bully Pulpit*, 748.

As he continued to tell the story, the Vice President for Products Trading walked through the trading floor. He was the manager's boss. He observed and heard the story, then immediately went up to the manager and said, "Stop this! I never want to see this again."

The manager immediately stopped. His expression changed from being a comic to embarrassment. The trading floor got quiet and we walked silently to the lunch room. The incident was never discussed, nor did I witness this troubling scene again.

Our Vice President could have simply walked away and said nothing. Instead, he chose to use his power publicly to right a wrong. The manager was a powerful person, yet was humbled by a more powerful person. All who witnessed this scene knew that mocking Africans was not acceptable in our business. Discrimination would not be tolerated. This taught me that power could be used effectively to change society for the better. I vowed to follow the Vice President's effective use of power if I ever obtained power.

Balancing Power

How do Christian workers balance the good and corrupt "double-sided sword" of power? Staying on the sidelines is always an easy option, but this leaves workers powerless and prone to abuses. When we are in leadership positions or have the chance to influence others through speaking and writing, we can give people a power platform that can make a positive impact to society, but this also exposes leaders to possible corruption.

The first step in balancing power is realizing that your power does not come from you; it was given by God and is limited. We live in this world for a short time. Once Christians look at the absolute power of God, they will quickly realize that there is no comparison between human power and God's power. We should use our limited power prudently in the workplace, looking to the Holy Spirit for guidance and skillfully using our competencies to positively impact our communities. Eventually, our workplace power will vanish when we retire or lose our jobs.[9] I have witnessed the panic and loss of identity in leaders who lose their power. Eventually, death will cause all our worldly powers to be gone. But Christians believe in the power of the resurrection: death is not the end.

Second, we need a supportive community surrounding us to serve as a sounding board. Friends, family, church members, and trusted co-workers

9. Parmiter, *Ten at Work*, 153–54.

are the best places to build this power-balancing community. These trusted individuals must be able to bluntly (with love) advise you when your power is getting out of balance. They should not care about your position. This is not a foolproof method, as there are occasions when your supportive community may not fully inform you of your negative behaviors. Other methods should then be employed.

When I was managing the North Region, I asked Doug, a human resource professional and an excellent developer of people, to devise a 360-feedback report on me by interviewing managers, peers, and professionals who knew me well. I wanted an anonymous composite of their feedback. Previously, I had sought feedback directly, but I believed that my leadership position kept people from telling me the full truth. When Doug showed me the 360 results, it opened my eyes to issues I needed to develop. Doug was direct, but also fair and factual. I developed a list of action items to address my deficiencies. By anonymously seeking feedback, my power was tabled and I received feedback with less filtering.

Third, we need to understand that power is addictive. The more power you are given, the more balancing is required. I recommend starting each day by reading the Bible or a devotional book to center your mind on God's power, not your own. Pray daily for wisdom from the Holy Spirit. Sit down with your spouse or trusted friend and ask, "Is the power I have corrupting me? Has my increased power changed me for the worse?" Look for changed patterns of power entitlements: spending, relationships, word choices, time allocations, service, etc.

If you lost your power, would your ego miss the power like a drug addict misses a fix? I have counseled a few professionals who struggled with the decision to retire. Some were afraid to leave Shell, as the workplace power had defined them. We would talk about "life after Shell," and their personal goals and competencies. I would encourage them to open up about what really worried them. It usually boiled down to the fear of change and starting something new. I was perplexed when highly motivated and competent employees with ample retirement funds would panic about it. Their identity was so wrapped up in their work.[10]

Power must be balanced. It is needed to be effective at work, but it should not define Christians. In fact, only by feeling joy without power, knowing that we are made in the image of God, can we lead effectively when we're given power. Richard Rohr states it like this:

10. Pfeffer, *Power*, 196–97.

> It seems to me that the only people who can handle power are those who don't need it too much, those who can equally let go of it and share it. In fact, I'd say that at this difficult moment in history, the only people who can handle power are those who have made journeys through *powerlessness*.[11]

With the growth in technology, it is even more important to understand power and institute checks and balances. By faithfully accepting that humans were made in God's image and that God commanded humans to be good stewards, Christians in the workplace can hold power responsibly. In our modern society, there are enough nuclear bombs to destroy our earth. Being faithful stewards in God's image comes with more responsibilities now than at any time since human creation. "To gain power over nature is now no longer the problem. But to use this power responsibly *for* nature and *for* a human future for man is the problem of the present day."[12]

To *Balance Power*, leaders must understand that power is a double-edged sword—it can be used to move our community toward the new creation or backward toward destruction. Power is addictive, and we are prone to power addiction. We must institute power checks and balances into our daily work lives to curb possible power abuses. Then Christians can use power effectively to help others achieve self-actualization, foster community, and advance the new creation.

After *Honor the Sabbath, Master Competence, Manage God's Providence, Exhibit Christlike Character, Practice Servant Leadership*, and *Balance Power*, we reach for the pinnacle, the seventh step of working Christians: *Be Missional*. What started as a small gathering of disciples following the teachings of a resurrected Jewish rabbi was eventually transformed into the largest global religion. To *Be Missional* is as relevant today as it was 2,000 years ago.

11. Rohr and Morrell, *Divine Dance*, 96 (emphasis Rohr's).
12. Moltmann, *On Human Being*, 110–11 (emphasis his).

Step 7: Be Missional

> *Christians are sent into the world to be*
> *faithful witnesses to the resurrected Christ.*
> *We are to be externally focused.*

The answer to the crisis of the North American church will not be found
at the level of method and problem solving. We share the conviction of a growing
consensus of Christians in North America that the problem is much more deeply
rooted. It has to do with who we are and what we are for. The real issues in the
current crisis of the Christian church are spiritual and theological.[1]

—*Published Committee Report—Missional Church:*
A Vision for the Sending of the Church in North America

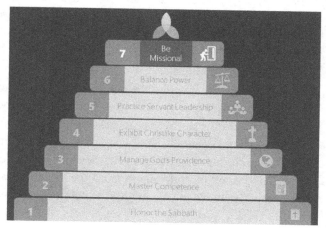

Figure 22—Step 7: Be Missional

1. Guder, *Missional Church*, 3.

WHEN SOMEONE SPEAKS ABOUT *missions*, we usually think about mission-aries going to remote places to evangelize and spread the gospel. Going on a mission trip implies a group of Christians traveling, near and far, to show their Christian faith in action by helping another community. A mission church is usually one built in an area where evangelism is the primary focus.

To *Be Missional* is more than planting churches, serving your neighbors, or evangelizing. It is about *sending*. It is about becoming *externally* focused. The church was founded through mission but, more importantly, the church must be missional—an alternative community. Christians are to be sent out of the church into the external world to self-actualize, positively impact their communities, and move our world toward the new creation. The church is and always has been people sent on a mission.[2] It is not a stopping place, but a starting place to spring into our community and transform it. Christians are not meant to withdraw into the sheltered life of the church to permanently escape the world. We are to engage with our surrounding culture, but not be controlled by that culture.[3] As writer Dorothy Sayers says, "It is not the business of the Church to adapt Christ to men, but to adapt men to Christ."[4]

Christianity is always a few generations from extinction; but being missional renews the church each generation. It has been this way since Christ gave the Great Commission to his disciples:

> And Jesus came and said to them, "All authority in heaven and on earth has been given to me. Go therefore and make disciples of all nations, baptizing them in the name of the Father and of the Son and of the Holy Spirit, and teaching them to obey everything that I have commanded you. And remember, I am with you always, to the end of the age" (Matt 28:18–20).

After Christ's resurrection, the gospel spread quickly within a pagan world, even during periods of Christian persecution. When it became the official religion of the Roman Empire during the fourth century CE, Christianity developed into a powerful institution. The once-persecuted majority Christian state then started persecuting the minority non-Christians to control religious beliefs. The Protestant Reformation and the Enlightenment ushered in new concepts founded on theological scholarship and scientific

2. Guder, *Missional Church*, 81.
3. Guder, *Missional Church*, 114.
4. Sayers, *Creed or Chaos?*, 36.

discoveries. Over time, church and state separated. World missions spread Christianity to all parts of our planet. After World War II, the European and American Christian populations started to erode. The "senders" of the gospel started rejecting mainstream Christianity. Western Christianity is now in decline.

Declining Western Christianity

According to the US Census Bureau, the population of the United States in 1960 was 180 million, within an estimated world population of 3 billion (6 percent). In 2018, the Census Bureau estimated US population at 328 million, and the world population at 7.5 billion (4.4 percent).[5] The US population has increased during my lifetime by 83 percent. World population has grown even faster (149 percent).

In contrast to the growth in US population, US Christianity has declined, both in percent of the population and in absolute numbers. This decline is a relatively new phenomenon in our nation's religious history. We are a country founded on religious freedom that established hundreds of thousands of Christian churches, hospitals, and educational institutions during the past 200-plus years as the United States expanded westward.

In 2015, the Pew Research Center published its 2014 US Religious Landscape Study that surveyed over 35,000 US adults. This was the second instance of this large survey; the first came in 2007. The report is detailed and statistically conclusive. The US adult (18 and older) Christian population is in decline. It is a sobering report:

> The percentage of adults (ages 18 and older) who describe themselves as Christians has dropped by nearly eight percentage points [-7.8 percent] in just seven years, from 78.4% in an equally massive Pew Research survey in 2007 to 70.6% in 2014. Over the same period, the percentage of Americans who are religiously unaffiliated—describing themselves as atheist, agnostic or "nothing in particular"—has jumped more than six points [+6.7 percent], from 16.1% to 22.8%.[6]

> In 2007, there were 227 million adults in the United States, and a little more than 78% of them—or roughly 178 million—identified as Christians. Between 2007 and 2014, the overall size of the US

5. "Population Clock."
6. Pew Research Center, "America's Changing Religious Landscape," 3.

adult population grew by about 18 million people, to nearly 245 million. But the share of adults who identify as Christians fell to just under 71%, or approximately 173 million Americans, a net decline of about 5 million.[7]

This is the current state of Christianity in the United States. Also in the Pew Research report:

> The drop in the Christian share of the population has been driven mainly by declines among mainline Protestants and Catholics [-3.4 percent and -3.1 percent].[8]

> In 2007, there were an estimated 41 million mainline Protestant adults in the United States. As of 2014, there are roughly 36 million, a decline of 5 million—although, taking into account the surveys' combined margins of error, the number of mainline Protestants may have fallen by as few as 3 million or as many as 7.3 million between 2007 and 2014.[9]

In my mainline Protestant denomination, the United Methodist Church (UMC), the Pew Research Report showed a decline from 5.1 percent of the 2007 US adult population to 3.6 percent in 2014 (-1.5 percent).[10] My Austin UMC church's membership has remained relatively stable over this period, a highly touted statistic given that the majority of UMC churches have declining memberships. When I was growing up in the 1960s and 1970s, churches had growing memberships that reflected the growing population.

While other faiths (non-Christians) have increased in the US adult population since 2007 (+1.2 percent), the largest population growth change is in the Unaffiliated, from 16.1 percent in 2007 to 22.8 percent in 2014, (+6.7 percent).[11] The research continues: "There are now approximately 56 million religiously unaffiliated adults in the US, and this group—sometimes called religious 'nones'—is more numerous than either Catholics or mainline Protestants."[12]

It is important to note that Pew adds, "Many people who are unaffiliated with a religion believe in God, pray at least occasionally, and think of

7. Pew Research Center, "America's Changing Religious Landscape," 7.

8. Pew Research Center, "America's Changing Religious Landscape," 4.

9. Pew Research Center, "America's Changing Religious Landscape," 8.

10. Pew Research Center, "America's Changing Religious Landscape," 21.

11. Pew Research Center, "America's Changing Religious Landscape," 3.

12. Pew Research Center, "America's Changing Religious Landscape," 10.

themselves as spiritual people."[13] The report goes on to add that "the un-affiliated are comparatively young—and getting *younger*, on average, over time." However, the mainline Protestant adults are growing older.[14] This is visibly evident when I attend my mainline church, as the members in the pews are older, on average, than the general population. Young adults and the number of children attending church are declining.

European Christianity declined earlier than North American Christianity. Bishop Lesslie Newbigin (1909–1998) left the United Kingdom in 1936 to serve in India and remained there until 1974. When he returned to the UK, he realized that missionary work was now needed in Western Christianity. I spent over nine years living and working in Europe between 1994 and 2014. We regularly worshipped in London and The Hague. When we traveled on the weekends, we usually attended worship services in cathedrals. These magnificent structures in once predominantly Christian communities were almost void of Sunday worshippers. The services were conducted in side chapels or the choir due to the small Sunday attendance. Those few attending were older, and we rarely saw young adults or children. The worship services were well organized with excellent choral music and preaching. The surrounding population simply did not attend the services.

It was in Europe that I first experienced negativity toward Christianity. Some of my office coworkers made jokes about Christians. When I announced that I was retiring and enrolling in a seminary to study theology, my Hamburg (Germany) manager said openly to my leadership team, "Why are you doing this? Just study philosophy!"

The declining Christian population is evident in seminaries. Once the top liberal arts students vied for entrance into the best seminaries. Pastors were viewed as community leaders and were respected for their scholarship and vocational choice. The expanding US population and geography created a shortage of educated ministers. The post-World War II growth of suburban communities included the construction of many new churches, which provided a steady market for ordained ministers. Now, seminary graduates must work hard to find ministerial positions. The membership declines correlate to fewer financial resources to pay for professional clergy. Supply and demand affect the church just as in capital markets.

---

13. Pew Research Center, "America's Changing Religious Landscape," 10.

14. Pew Research Center, "America's Changing Religious Landscape," 5–6.

Four Primary Purposes of the Church

There are four primary purposes of the church: community worship, prayer, discipleship, and service. A community of Christians gathers together as a church to worship, pray, grow in faith, and serve the community. If one or more of these four activities is missing, then the church will not reach its full potential. If other activities are added, the core activities of a church are diluted, making membership declines more likely. A church is a needed community of high standards of conduct, says founder of Focused Community Strategies Urban Ministries Robert Lupton: "The church remains the primary guardian of moral and ethical values." [15] Churches are composed of imperfect people who strive to improve communities.

When a Christian church looks and acts like the unchurched, it is no longer an alternative community; it is just another community center. When an unchurched person drives past a church and sees a building but has no idea about its role in the community, the church faces a market share competition with nonreligious community programs. A church that is internally focused rather than being missional is headed for decline over time. Without Christians *leaving* the internal church for the vast majority of their week, Christianity will decline. The church is the entire community (churched and nonchurched), not a building or the members of a congregation. A missional church listens to the Holy Spirit and follows God in mission. Missional churches ask the primary question: "What is God doing in our community?"

It is my opinion that one of the major reasons for declining US (and European) Christianity is that most Christian churches are not preparing Christians for life outside the church buildings. Churches are not being missional.

Four Deficiencies of the Church

Why is this so? There are four deficiencies that need to be rectified.

The first deficiency is that churches are not equipping Christians for service in the workplace. Rev. Timothy Keller writes, "Most pastors were more concerned about helping us [Christians] serve inside the church than about discipling and equipping us to serve in the world."[16]

---

15. Lupton, *Toxic Charity*, 68.
16. Keller, *Every Good Endeavor*, xviii.

I've been a member of various mainline Protestant churches since my teenage confirmation. Only one, Holy Trinity Brompton in London, offered a class in work and faith (*God at Work*, authored by Ken Costa, a London investment banker). The church is just not equipping their community for external work, and work is where most of the community is spending the majority of their time. Work and faith are rarely discussed.

In church, we worship our Creator, Redeemer, and Sustainer. We pray to God as a community of faith with words of praise, gratitude, confession, and petition. In discipleship, we grow individually to prepare for our mission in the external workplace community. Gregory Pierce, president of Catholic ACTA Publications, says, "The workplace is in fact exactly where the great majority of us are supposed to carry out our Christian mission."[17] However, our employers don't pay us to evangelize other employees.[18] Christians also should be working for self-actualization, service to our community, and the coming new creation. We are not in the workplace to push our religious beliefs on our fellow employees. Our actions will speak louder than our proselytizing. And when in a leadership position, evangelizing subordinate employees is a misuse of power. Let the Holy Spirit work in the workplace as others observe our Christian Sabbath practices, competency, character, stewardship, management style, and use of power. Our daily walk with Christ will be a shining light in our workplace.

The second deficiency is that many pastors are not trained or experienced in the workplace outside the institutional church, although this may change over time as more second-career workers enter seminary. My seminary class had students who had been lawyers, teachers, government employees, and engineers. These experienced workers didn't downgrade their former occupations, but used their professional experiences to relate to those in the community. Seminaries equip their students to serve in the church through leading worship, teaching, preaching, and counseling, but there were no classes on work and faith—at least not at my seminary. If a pastor's professional life is spent only within the church, then it will be difficult to focus the congregation externally. When was the last time you saw a minister visiting the workplace? When was the last time you heard a sermon on faith and work?

Some have offered an even more radical idea. In the 1876 publication of George MacDonald's (1824–1905) novel, *The Curate's Awakening*, he offers a stunning proposition: clergy must first prove capable of making a

17. Pierce, *Finding God@Work*, 29.

18. Costa, *God at Work*, 44.

living in another calling and not be "ordained till after forty, by which time he would know whether he had any real call or only a temptation to the church from the hope of an easy living."[19] While this idea is too constraining for those called to ministry, and professional ministry is certainly not always easy living, some external experience would help church professionals relate better to their congregations.

To balance this idea, perhaps the training should go both ways, as workers need to understand the impact of their work on their communities. An excellent proposal was written by Mark S. Markuly, Dean of the School of Theology and Ministry at Seattle University, that allows theology and business students to better understand each other. Theology students should intern in corporate settings to be exposed to complex business relationships, commercial decision-making, and difficult employment choices. Business students should intern in social service agencies "seeing first-hand the effects of economic deprivation." They should spend time with community leaders and workers who have lost their jobs and adults who work multiple minimum-wage jobs. They need to visit with families of hospitalized children who lack adequate medical insurance to understand their stress. "Wizened by the human pain caused by the economic system, business students will have a better starting point in their discussions with religious leaders and theologians who increasingly use the poor and marginalized as a point of departure for their thinking about issues of economics."[20] Both can learn from each other.

The third deficiency is that laypersons need to be more involved in the church. According to authors Doug Sherman and William Hendricks:

> The model of congregational life in the minds of most clergy and laity is one in which the minister is a dominant pastoral superstar who specializes in the spiritual concerns of the Christian community, while the laity are spectators, critics and recipients of pastoral care, free to go about their own business because the pastor is taking care of the business of the kingdom.[21]

The pastor and staff should not be the focus of a church. Laypersons should lead worship, read Scripture, make announcements, preach, lead community prayers, teach, and serve. They should develop their leadership skills and Christian competencies within the church. With more

19. MacDonald, *Curate's Awakening*, 189–90.

20. See Mark S. Markuly, in Capaldi, *Business and Religion*, 38–39.

21. Sherman and Hendricks, *Your Work Matters to God*, 222.

lay participation, church expenses will be reduced, as fewer professional church staff members are required. This would reduce the gap between the secular and sacred worlds. If we don't restore "the layperson to a front-line status in the cause of Christ, . . . we as Christians are rapidly conceding the field, with the result that the workplace grows more unholy, while the Church grows more irrelevant."[22]

The fourth deficiency is that churches are called to serve the community effectively and efficiently. Competent working Christians with strategic skills are needed for service to the community. A church should welcome these workplace skills. Far too often, church service projects are carried out with heartfelt enthusiasm and sadly, poor use of resources—both human and financial. Robert D. Lupton wrote *Toxic Charity* about the problems with charity work and proposed guidelines for compassionate community service:

- Never do for the poor what they have (or could have) the capacity to do for themselves.

- Limit one-way giving to emergency situations.

- Strive to empower the poor through employment, lending, and investing, using grants sparingly to reinforce achievements.

- Subordinate self-interests to the needs of those being served.

- Listen closely to those you seek to help, especially to what is not being said—unspoken feelings may contain essential clues to effective service.

- Above all, do no harm.[23]

Lupton adds, "We miss the big picture because we view aid through the narrow lens of the needs of *our* organization or church—focusing on what will benefit *our* team the most—and neglecting the best interests of those we would serve."[24]

I learned through experience and study that some compassionate service work could be better executed. These are some of my recommendations:

22. Sherman and Hendricks, *Your Work Matters to God*, 237.
23. Lupton, *Toxic Charity*, 8–9.
24. Lupton, *Toxic Charity*, 15 (emphasis his).

1. The ultimate service goal should enable the served to be self-sufficient within a projected timeline. The server facilitates the served gaining self-sufficiency.

2. The majority of all financial and human resources should go to those served. This includes all travel expenses, financial giving, materials, and human service time.

3. The served must first be understood through bonding with them in community and listening deeply. This process can take years before the implementation of service work, but greatly increases the probability of success.

4. The service project should be long-term-focused with a strategic plan that is developed after the investigation phase and before implementation. The plan should be updated regularly as the project evolves.

5. The service should be bidirectional: The served should also serve the server as they are able.

My experience with church service work has been tainted by far too many well-intended but nonstrategic and poorly implemented service projects. The serving hearts were in the right place, but many were just giving goods to fix conditions that were not life-threatening, thus encouraging entitlements and dependencies, and did not uplift the community to self-sufficiency. Christians are called to give our resources of time, talent, and finances to others in need. Those suffering tragic natural disasters, starvation, disease, and unjust conditions must be helped. The immediate life-threatening conditions must be eliminated. Christ taught us to serve our neighbors. But our goal should also be to enable our neighbors to be self-sufficient and not to create entitlement nor establish dependency.[25] Our hearts *and* minds must be at work when we give.

The goal should be for the server's job to be eliminated after a period of training and resourcing. It would be far better for churches to encourage their members to serve in effective nonprofits than to implement nonstrategic, ineffective, and inefficient services to the community. Sometimes tension builds between church members who ask hard questions (covering the need for the service work, effective guidelines, and strategic goals) and the compassionate volunteers involved. This is why some church members

25. Lupton, *Toxic Charity*, 130.

work with strategic nonprofits rather than work to change ineffective church services. We should connect compassionate hearts with an effective strategy. My hope is that with education, the church will become truly missional. Time is running against Western Christian churches, and prompt changes are required.

As Christians, we are called to *Be Missional*, which means going out into the world. The workplace is a fertile missional location. It is where most Christians spend the majority of their time. Christians are needed in the workplace to reverse the declining Christianity trend. Escaping the world by insular activities is not missional. A church friend once told me that he spends all his nonworking time on church activities: Bible study, men's group, singing in the choir, directing Sunday morning traffic, committee meetings, etc. I asked why he did so many church activities. He said that he felt uncomfortable around non-Christians and preferred to be with Christians. While I commend his devoted service to the church, this is one of the reasons why Christianity is in decline. The missional church entails going out of your church building into the workplace, the unchurched community, nonprofits, government—*the world*. Bob Buford, co-founder of the Halftime Institute, which equips Christian leaders, says:

> People need to *see* our faith, not merely hear about it. When our beliefs are personal and privatized, practiced only inside a building one day a week, we Christians miss out on that glorious opportunity to be salt and light. Worse, I believe that when faith continues to be directed inward, we become one-dimensional, uninteresting, and wholly self-centered persons. We have a work life, a family life, a community life, and a church life. And when segregated like that, each sphere is less robust than it could be.[26]

Let your Christian faith shine in the office, in the classroom, in the plant, at the construction site, on the road, in an airplane, in the military, in the hospital, in a nonprofit, on the water, on the sports field, in the home, and in church. Our Christian lifestyle should be so distinctive that our coworkers will seek to know about it. *Be Missional* and Christians will revert to what made early Christianity so successful—achieving self-actualization, serving the community, and working toward the new creation.

---

26. Buford, *Half Time*, 166 (emphasis his).

Final Comments

I suggest that we have come to the day of the layperson, the day when the key operative in the Church is not a pope or a saint or a monk or an evangelist or a missionary or even a "highly committed" churchman—but the everyday worker who simply puts Christ first in his or her career, as in the rest of life.[1]

—DOUG SHERMAN, PRESIDENT AND FOUNDER OF CAREER IMPACT MINISTRIES

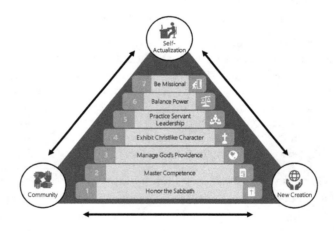

Figure 23—Integrating Your Faith into Your Work

I SERVE ON THE Southwestern University Board of Trustees. My daughter and son-in-law graduated from this liberal arts university located in Georgetown, Texas. During their years of attendance and afterwards, I grew in my relationship with this UMC-affiliated educational institution.

---

1. Sherman and Hendricks, *Your Work Matters to God*, 269.

Every year or two, the university hosts the Roy & Margaret Shilling Lecture Series. Past lecturers have included diverse and esteemed speakers such as former President Jimmy Carter, Archbishop Desmond Tutu, writer Thomas Friedman, and naturalist Jane Goodall.

My wife and I drove to Georgetown for a Board of Trustees dinner and the 2018 Shilling Lecture. The lecturer that evening was Dr. Jonathan Haidt, a social psychologist and expert in the psychology of morality. Dr. Haidt is the Thomas Cooley Professor of Ethical Leadership at New York University's Stern School of Business. Before that evening, I had never heard of Dr. Haidt or moral psychology.

Dr. Haidt's lecture was titled "The Age of Outrage: What It Is Doing to Our Universities and Our Country." Dr. Haidt is an excellent scholar and an outstanding speaker. He spoke about the current divisions in the United States and showed his and others' research about why these divisions exist. He has grown increasingly pessimistic on the future direction of our country, but offered several suggestions to rectify these divisions. My wife and I drove home that evening in vigorous discussion about what we had heard that evening. The subsequent Southwestern University Board retreat included Dr. Haidt's topic, and I heard many of my fellow Trustees and the Southwestern administration express their opinions on his lecture topic.

I decided to read more of Dr. Haidt's work. To be transparent, Dr. Haidt was raised Jewish but professes that he is now a liberal atheist. He is a scientist who relies on factual research to explain human behavior. I purchased his acclaimed book, *The Righteous Mind: Why Good People Are Divided by Politics and Religion.* I began reading it and, with each page, my mind tried to grasp moral psychology and the vast amount of research in this field. I read a section titled "Three Ethics are More Descriptive Than One."[2] Dr. Haidt describes a new theory of morality developed by Richard A. Shweder, Professor of Human Development at the University of Chicago. Shweder is a psychological anthropologist. What surprised me was that moral ethics research clusters around three themes: autonomy, community, and divinity, which are all integral parts of my model.

The first ethic, autonomy, is founded upon the individual:

> The ethic of *autonomy* is based on the idea that people are, first and foremost, autonomous individuals with wants, needs, and preferences. People should be free to satisfy these wants, needs, and preferences as they see fit, and so societies develop moral

2. Haidt, *Righteous Mind,* 115–18.

concepts such as rights, liberty, and justice, which allow people
to coexist peacefully without interfering too much in each other's
projects. This is the dominant ethic in individualistic societies.[3]

This closely corresponds to self-actualization in my theological model of
work. Humans are created in the image of God and strive for self-actualization. Maslow proposed that humans have needs ranging from physiological
to self-actualization. One way to achieve self-actualization is through our
work.

The second ethic revolves around our community:

> The ethic of *community* is based on the idea that people are, first
> and foremost, members of larger entities such as families, teams,
> armies, companies, tribes, and nations. These larger entities are
> more than the sum of the people who compose them; they are real,
> they matter, and they must be protected. People have an obliga-
> tion to play their assigned roles in these entities. Many societies
> therefore develop moral concepts such as duty, hierarchy, respect,
> reputation, and patriotism. In such societies, the Western insis-
> tence that people should design their own lives and pursue their
> own goals seems selfish and dangerous—a sure way to weaken the
> social fabric and destroy the institutions and collective entities
> upon which everyone depends.[4]

Community is the second part of my theological model of work. Jesus
Christ taught humanity how to live in community. We live in relationship
to one another. God created humans for community and instructed us to
be stewards of our precious earth. Community balances the destructive
tendencies of individualism (autonomy). We work for the benefit of all, not
just ourselves.

The third ethic is divinity:

> The ethic of *divinity* is based on the idea that people are, first and
> foremost, temporary vessels within which a divine soul has been
> implanted. People are not just animals with an extra serving of
> consciousness; they are children of God and should behave ac-
> cordingly . . . Many societies therefore develop moral concepts
> such as sanctity and sin, purity and pollution, elevation and deg-
> radation. In such societies, the personal liberty of secular Western

---

3. Haidt, *Righteous Mind*, 116 (emphasis his).
4. Haidt, *Righteous Mind*, 116–17 (emphasis his).

nations looks like libertinism, hedonism, and a celebration of humanity's baser instincts.[5]

Divinity relates to the new creation, the third part of my theological model of work. The Holy Spirit propels Christians toward the new creation through obedience to God. It is God who reveals through Scripture how Christians are to be obedient. Christians are to use their God-given individual gifts, within community, to establish the reign of God. During our short time on this planet, we are to be good stewards of God's creation for future generations to enjoy. What we do today in our work matters for the future.

Shweder bases the three morality ethics on his research. Dr. Haidt describes the three ethics separately and implies relative independence. I see the three as balanced, distinct, nonhierarchical, and interrelated. My theological model corresponds to the three persons of the Trinity. I based my theological model of work on Scripture, theological writings, and my own experiences in the working environment. I believe that humans are created in the image of God and made for community; therefore, I cannot separate divinity from the other two ethics. I find it fascinating that morality research roughly corresponds to my theological model of work.

My three-fold theological model of work can be put into practice whether at home caring for older or future generations, or at the workplace. I propose seven steps that build upon each other for working Christians to follow:

1. *Honor the Sabbath*—Remember the Sabbath day and keep it holy. Take a day to remove yourself from the world of space and rest in God's eternal world.

2. *Master Competence*—Be proficient at a skill by working hard and long to master it. Be competent in your religion, a faith seeking understanding.

3. *Manage God's Providence*—God provides, and we are God's stewards on earth. Manage God's resources effectively and benevolently within your workplace, home, and church.

4. *Exhibit Christlike Character*—Let your fellow workers see the light of Christ within you. Our character is founded upon humility, gratitude, and courage.

---

5. Haidt, *Righteous Mind*, 117 (emphasis his).

5. *Practice Servant Leadership*—The great leader is seen as a servant first. Our leadership skills come from God and are used to develop people and serve the community.

6. *Balance Power*—Power is a double-edged sword—both good and corrupt. Power is to be used for justice, to save lives, to serve the public's interest, and to move the community toward the new creation.

7. *Be Missional*: Christians are sent into the world to be faithful witnesses to the resurrected Christ. We are to be externally focused.

Placing this theological model of work into practice through these seven steps will enable your Christian faith to be relevant in the workplace. Faith and work are not two separate worlds, but are joined together. Work has meaning in a Christian's journey of faith. Back in 2011, I wished I could have more effectively answered Ian's question—"Can I work for Shell and still be a Christian?" The good news is that through the long journey of study and questioning, I now have a much better answer which I have shared with you in this book:

> *Work should enable self-actualization and uplift communities as workers follow the Holy Spirit toward the new creation.*

This is how Christians integrate faith and work.

Appendix A
Scriptural Graphs

Service Occupations	Old Testament	New Testament	Total
Servant	237	21	258
Eunuch	21	10	31
Maid	28	1	29
Steward	9	9	18
Courier	5	-	5
Total	300	41	341

Figure 24—Service Occupations

Government Occupations	Old Testament	New Testament	Total
Official	178	8	186
Governor	60	24	84
Scribe	22	62	84
Gatekeeper	38	-	38
Secretary	34	-	34
Councilor	28	1	29
Minister	15	10	25
Tax Collector	-	22	22
Recorder	9	-	9
Deputy	7	-	7
Treasurer	6	-	6
Prefect	5	-	5
Doorkeeper	2	1	3
Justice	2	-	2
Commissioner	1	-	1
Total	407	128	535

Figure 25—Government Occupations

Religious Occupations	Old Testament	New Testament	Total
Priest	779	168	947
Rabbi	-	15	15
Total	779	183	962

Figure 26—Religious Occupations

Artisan & Manufacturing Occupations	Old Testament	New Testament	Total
Artisan	27	2	29
Builder	12	12	24
Potter	21	2	23
Smith	14	-	14
Carpenter	9	2	11
Goldsmith	9	-	9
Weaver	8	-	8
Stonecutter	6	-	6
Mason	6	-	6
Designer	2	-	2
Embroiderer	2	-	2
Restorer	2	-	2
Silversmith	1	1	2
Caulker	1	-	1
Dresser	1	-	1
Engraver	1	-	1
Repairer	1	-	1
Tentmaker	-	1	1
Carder	1	-	1
Wielder	1	-	1
Total	125	20	145

Figure 27—Artisan and Manufacturing Occupations

Nautical Occupations	Old Testament	New Testament	Total
Pilot	4	2	6
Fisherman	1	3	4
Mariner	4	-	4
Total	9	5	14

Figure 28—Nautical Occupations

Leadership Occupations	Old Testament	New Testament	Total
Overseer	11	1	12
Taskmaster	9	-	9
Manager	-	8	8
Supervisor	6	-	6
Total	26	9	35

Figure 29—Leadership Occupations

Business & Professional Occupations	Old Testament	New Testament	Total
Teacher	14	69	83
Merchant	24	4	28
Trader	11	1	12
Debtor	3	3	6
Creditor	5	1	6
Seller	5	-	5
Buyer	4	-	4
Dealer	2	2	4
Purchaser	3	-	3
Borrower	2	-	2
Lender	2	-	2
Attorney	-	1	1
Total	75	81	156

Figure 30—Business and Professional Occupations

Musical & Visual Arts Occupations	Old Testament	New Testament	Total
Singer	39	-	39
Trumpeter	5	1	6
Musician	4	-	4
Dancer	2	-	2
Harpist	-	2	2
Minstrel	-	1	1
Flutist	-	1	1
Total	50	5	55

Figure 31—Musical and Visual Arts Occupations

Agricultural Work	Old Testament	New Testament	Total
Gather	80	16	96
Harvest	57	16	73
Sow	48	21	69
Plant	45	10	55
Reap	20	9	29
Glean	22	-	22
Hew	18	2	20
Plow	17	3	20
Tread	11	2	13
Till	12	-	12
Winnow	9	-	9
Grind	6	2	8
Dig	6	2	8
Prune	8	-	8
Thresh	6	2	8
Tend	4	2	6
Cut	4	-	4
Cultivate	1	2	3
Harrow	3	-	3
Ingathering	2	-	2
Seedtime	1	-	1
Irrigate	1	-	1
Total	381	89	470

Figure 32—Agricultural Work

Business-Related Work	Old Testament	New Testament	Total
Sale	107	51	158
Buy	65	27	92
Pay	52	25	77
Wage	28	10	38
Goods	31	5	36
Trade	22	8	30
Exchange	18	-	18
Profit	12	4	16
Market	2	14	16
Debt	7	7	14
Merchandise	14	-	14
Lend	9	4	13
Purchase	12	-	12
Borrow	8	2	10
Business	4	5	9
Wares	8	1	9
Fee	3	-	3
Barter	2	-	2
Credit	-	1	1
Total	404	164	568

Figure 33—Business-Related Work

Artisan & Manu-facturing Work	Old Testament	New Testament	Total
Repair	66	-	66
Rebuild	52	1	53
Cast	44	5	49
Carve	27	-	27
Restore	17	-	17
Embroider	16	-	16
Engrave	12	-	12
Dress	9	-	9
Design	2	-	2
Caulk	1	-	1
Stonecutting	1	-	1
Weaving	1	-	1
Total	248	6	254

Figure 34—Artisan and Manufacturing Work

Management & Government Work	Old Testament	New Testament	Total
Minister	33	-	33
Govern	10	1	11
Manage	-	5	5
Oversee	1	-	1
Total	44	6	50

Figure 35—Management and Government Work

Appendix B
Glossary of Theological Terms

Asceticism

Discipline that renounces desires or pleasures for the purpose of doing God's will.

Charis

Greek word for grace. Unmerited favor. God's undeserved grace is extended to sinful humanity by providing salvation and forgiveness through Jesus Christ, while the judgment that is deserved is withheld.

Christology

The study of the person and work of Jesus Christ.

Dialectic Theology

A theological movement, associated with Karl Barth and others, stressing the paradoxical nature of divine truths. For example, thus is God both grace and judgment.

Dogma

A teaching or doctrine which has received an official church status as truth.

Eschatology

The study of the last things, or the end of the world, which includes the second coming of Jesus Christ and the last judgment.

Faith Seeking Understanding

A phrase used to describe theology. It can be a scientific, methodical attempt to understand God's divine revelation.

Gratitude

The response to God and God's blessings that is an expression of praise and devotion.

Hermit

One who lives in solitude (often in the desert), withdrawn from the world out of religious conviction.

Kairos

Greek term for time, denoting a special, significantly critical point in human history when God's will and purposes are carried out, particularly in the coming of Jesus Christ.

Kingdom of God

God's sovereign reign and rule. It is a major focus of Jesus' teachings. Equivalent phrases are "kingdom of Jesus" and "kingdom of heaven."

Liberal Theology

A theological movement, stemming from F. D. E. Schleiermacher, that sought to reformulate Christian doctrine in contemporary terms. It emphasized the use of reason, science, freedom, and experience while focusing on human goodness and the progress between the divine and humans.

Liberation Theologies

Various twentieth-century theological movements that see the gospel as liberation from all forms of oppression (economic, spiritual, political, and social).

Moral Character

One's basic disposition or nature with regard to questions of right and wrong morality.

197

New Creation	The anticipated renewal of the created order by God in the "new heaven and new earth" as found in Revelation 21:1, Romans 8:18–21, and 2 Peter 3:13.
Ontology	The philosophical study of being as being. It is thus the study of the underlying principles that are present in all things that exist solely by virtue of their existing.
Parousia	A Greek term used for the "coming of Christ," most usually focused on the second coming.
Pneumatology	The theological study of the Holy Spirit.
Protology	The study of the revealed doctrine of first things, or the beginning of the world.
Sanctification	The process or result of God's continuing work in Christian believers through the power of the Holy Spirit.
Scholastic Theology	The theology of the schools used to designate the formal theology of the medieval period marked by a heavy use of logic, reliance upon philosophical concepts, and linguistic precision. Its goal is to present a systematic ordering and investigation of Christian truths.
Systematic Theology	A branch of Christian theology that attempts to present theological thinking and practice in an orderly and coherent way.
Theology	The study of God. It is a language or discourse about God. It is also known as faith seeking understanding.

Bibliography

"2013 Church Budget Allocations, Learning Priorities, and Quarterly Financial Trends." https://danieldailey.files.wordpress.com/2015/07/eccu_2013_church_budget_trends.pdf.

Aquinas, Thomas. *Summa Theologica*, vol. II. New York: Benziger Brothers, 1947.

———. *Summa Theologica*. vol. III. New York: Benziger Brothers, 1948.

Augustine, Saint. *A Select Library of the Nicene and Post-Nicene Fathers of the Christian Church*. Vol. III. Edited by Philip Schaff. Grand Rapids: Eerdmans, 1956.

Bakke, Dennis W. *Joy at Work: A Revolutionary Approach to Fun on the Job*. Toronto: Viking, 2005.

Banks, Robert J. *Faith Goes to Work: Reflections from the Marketplace*. New York: The Alban Institute, 1993.

Barrett, Lois Y., et al., eds. *Treasure in Clay Jars: Patterns in Missional Faithfulness*. Grand Rapids: Eerdmans, 2004.

Barth, Karl. *Church Dogmatics: A Selection With Introduction by Helmut Gollwitzer*. 14 vols. Louisville, KY: Westminster John Knox, 1961.

———. *Church Dogmatics: The Doctrine of Creation*, vol. III. Edinburgh: T. & T. Clark, 1961.

———. *The Word of God and the Word of Man*. Gloucester, MA: Peter Smith, 1978.

Baum, Gregory. *The Priority of Labor: A Commentary on Laborem Exercens, Encyclical Letter of Pope John Paul II*. New York: Paulist, 1982.

Beckett, John D. *Mastering Monday: A Guide to Integrating Faith and Work*. Downers Grove, IL: InterVarsity, 2006.

Bolt, John. *Economic Shalom: A Reformed Primer on Faith, Work, and Human Flourishing*. Grand Rapids: Christian's Library, 2013.

Branson, Roy. "Sabbath—Heart of Jewish Unity." *Journal of Ecumenical Studies* 15.4 (Fall 1978) 716–36.

Brooks, David. *The Road to Character*. New York: Random House, 2015.

Brueggemann, Walter. *Sabbath as Resistance: Saying NO to the Culture of Now*. Louisville, KY: Westminster John Knox, 2014.

Buford, Bob. *Half Time: Moving from Success to Significance*. Grand Rapids: Zondervan, 2008.

Calvin, John. *Institutes of the Christian Religion*. Translated by Henry Beveridge. Peabody, MA: Hendrickson, 2008.

Capaldi, Nicholas, ed. *Business and Religion: A Clash of Civilizations?* Salem, MA: M & M Scrivener, 2005.

Caro, Robert A. *The Years of Lyndon Johnson: The Passage of Power*. New York: Vintage, 2013.

Carr, David M. *An Introduction to the Old Testament: Sacred Texts and Imperial Contexts of the Hebrew Bible*. Malden, MA: John Wiley & Sons, 2010.

Cavanaugh, William T. *Being Consumed: Economics and Christian Desire*. Grand Rapids: Eerdmans, 2008.

Chrysostom, John. *A Select Library of the Nicene and Post-Nicene Fathers of the Christian Church*, vol. IX. Edited by Philip Schaff. Grand Rapids: Eerdmans, 1956.

"Church Budget Priorities Survey: Executive Report." https://www.christianitytoday.com/special/ycresources/pdf/exec-report_churchbudgetpriorities.pdf.

Comfort, Philip, and Walter A. Elwell. *The Complete Book of Who's Who in the Bible*. New York: Castle, 2014.

Cosden, Darrell. *A Theology of Work: Work and the New Creation*. Eugene, OR: Wipf and Stock, 2006.

Costa, Ken. *God at Work: Living Every Day With Purpose*. London: Continuum, 2007.

Dalberg-Acton, John. "Letter to Archbishop Mandell Creighton: April 5, 1887." https://history.hanover.edu/courses/excerpts/165acton.html.

Diehl, William E. *The Monday Connection: On Being an Authentic Christian in a Weekday World*. Eugene, OR: Wipf and Stock, 2012.

Duckworth, Angela. *Grit: The Power of Passion and Perseverance*. New York: Scribner, 2016.

Figgis, John Neville, and Reginald Vere Laurence, eds. *Historical Essays and Studies*. London: Macmillan, 1907.

Fox, Matthew. *The Reinvention of Work: A New Vision of Livelihood for Our Time*. New York: HarperOne, 1994.

God's Work in Our Hands: Employment, Community, and Christian Vocation. Louisville, KY: The Office of the General Assembly, 1995.

González, Justo L. *The Story of Christianity*, vol. I. New York: HarperCollins, 2010.

————. *The Story of Christianity*, vol. II. New York: HarperCollins, 2010.

Goodwin, Doris Kearns. *The Bully Pulpit: Theodore Roosevelt and the Golden Age of Journalism*. London: Viking, 2013.

Green, Arthur. *Judaism's 10 Best Ideas: A Brief Guide for Seekers*. Woodstock, VT: Jewish Lights, 2014.

Greene, Mark. *Thank God it's Monday: Ministry in the Workplace*. Bletchley, UK: Scripture Union, 2002.

Greenleaf, Robert K. *Servant Leadership: A Journey into the Nature of Legitimate Power and Greatness*. Mahwah, NJ: Paulist, 2002.

Guder, Darrell L., ed. *Missional Church: A Vision for the Sending of the Church in North America*. Grand Rapids: Eerdmans, 1998.

Hage, Dean R., et al. *Money Matters: Personal Giving in American Churches*. Louisville, KY: Westminster John Knox, 1996.

Haidt, Jonathan. *The Righteous Mind: Why Good People are Divided by Politics and Religion*. New York: Vintage, 2013.

Hall, Douglass John. *The Steward: A Biblical Symbol Come of Age*. Rev. ed. Eugene, OR: Wipf and Stock, 2004.

Hart, Ian. "The Teaching of Luther and Calvin about Ordinary Work: 1. Martin Luther (1483–1546)." *Evangelical Quarterly* 67.1 (1995) 35–52.

———. "The Teaching of Luther and Calvin about Ordinary Work: 2. John Calvin (1509–64)." *Evangelical Quarterly* 67.2 (1995) 121–35.

———. "The Teaching of the Puritans about Ordinary Work." *Evangelical Quarterly* 67.3 (1995) 195–209.

Heschel, Abraham Joshua. *The Sabbath: Its Meaning for Modern Man.* New York: Farrar, Straus, and Giroux, 1951.

Hicks, Douglas A. *Religion and the Workplace: Pluralism, Spirituality, Leadership.* Cambridge: Cambridge University Press, 2003.

Jaffee, Martin S. *Early Judaism: Religious Worlds of the First Judaic Millennium.* Bethesda: University Press of Maryland, 2006.

Jensen, David H. *Responsive Labor: A Theology of Work.* Louisville, KY: Westminster John Knox, 2006.

Johnson, Luke Timothy. *Sharing Possessions: What Faith Demands.* 2nd ed. Grand Rapids: Eerdmans, 2011.

Kaiser, Edwin G. *Theology of Work.* Westminster, MD: Newman, 1966.

Keller, Timothy. *Every Good Endeavor: Connecting Your Work to God's Work.* New York: Riverhead, 2014.

Kroeger, Catherine Clark, trans. "John Chrysostom's First Homily on the Greeting to Priscilla and Aquila." *Priscilla Papers* 5.3 (Summer 1991) 16–20.

Larive, Armand. *After Sunday: A Theology of Work.* New York: Continuum International, 2004.

Lukes, Steven, ed. *Power.* New York: New York University Press, 1986.

Lupton, Robert D. *Toxic Charity: How Churches and Charities Hurt Those They Help (And How to Reverse it).* New York: HarperCollins, 2011.

Luther, Martin. *Luther's Works*, vol. 1. *Lectures on Genesis Chapters 1–5.* Edited by Jaroslav Pelikan. St. Louis: Concordia, 1958.

———. *Luther's Works*, vol. 2. *Lectures on Genesis.* Edited by Jaroslav Pelikan. St. Louis: Concordia, 1960.

———. *Luther's Works*, vol. 14. *Selected Psalms.* Edited by Jaroslav Pelikan and Daniel E. Poellot. St. Louis: Concordia, 1958.

———. *Luther's Works*, vol. 15. *Notes on Ecclesiastes.* Edited by Jaroslav Pelikan and Hilton C. Oswald. St. Louis: Concordia, 1972.

———. *Luther's Works*, vol. 21. *(Sermons) and the Magnificat.* Edited by Jaroslav Pelikan. St. Louis: Concordia, 1956.

———. *Luther's Works*, vol. 28. *Commentaries on I Corinthians.* Edited by Hilton C. Oswald. St. Louis: Concordia, 1973.

———. *Luther's Works*, vol. 30. *The Catholic Epistles.* Edited by Jaroslav Pelikan and Walter A. Hansen. St. Louis: Concordia, 1967.

———. *Luther's Works*, vol. 31. *Career of the Reformer: I.* Edited by Harold J. Grimm and Helmut T. Lehmann. Philadelphia: Fortress, 1957.

———. *Luther's Works*, vol. 36. *Word and Sacrament II.* Edited by Abdel Ross Wentz and Helmut T. Lehmann. Philadelphia: Fortress, 1959.

———. *Luther's Works*, vol. 44. *The Christian in Society I.* Edited by James Atkinson and Helmut T. Lehmann. Philadelphia: Fortress, 1966.

———. *Luther's Works*, vol. 45. *The Christian in Society II.* Edited by Walther I. Brandt and Helmut T. Lehmann. Philadelphia: Fortress, 1962.

———. *Luther's Works*, vol. 46. *The Christian in Society III.* Edited by Robert C. Schultz and Helmut T. Lehmann. Philadelphia: Fortress, 1967.

MacDonald, George. *The Curate's Awakening*. Minneapolis: Bethany House, 1985.

Maslow, A. H. *A Theory of Human Motivation*. Mansfield Center, CT: Martino, 2013.

———. "A Theory of Human Motivation." *Psychological Review* 50 (1943) 370–96.

McKim, Donald K. *Westminster Dictionary of Theological Terms*. Louisville, KY: Westminster John Knox, 1996.

Memorial Drive Presbyterian Church. "Our Story: Dollar-for-Dollar Giving." http://www.mdpc.org/about-us/our-story/.

Michelson, A. Elihu. "Toward a Guide for Jewish Ritual Usage: Part IV – The Sabbath and Dietary Usages." *The Reconstructionist* 7.16 (1941) 10–17.

Moltmann, Jürgen. *The Coming of God: Christian Eschatology*. Translated by Margaret Kohl. Minneapolis: Fortress, 2004.

———. *God in Creation: A New Theology of Creation and the Spirit of God*. Translated by Margaret Kohl. Minneapolis: Fortress, 1993.

———. *On Human Being: Christian Anthropology in the Conflicts of the Present*. Translated by John Sturdy. Minneapolis: Fortress, 2009.

———. *On Human Dignity: Political Theology and Ethics*. Translated by M. Douglas Meeks. Philadelphia: Fortress, 1984.

———. *Theology of Hope: On the Ground and the Implications of a Christian Eschatology*. Translated by James W. Leitch. Minneapolis: Fortress, 1993.

———. *Theology of Play*. Translated by Reinhard Ulrich. New York: Harper & Row, 1972.

———. *The Way of Jesus Christ: Christology in Messianic Dimensions*. Translated by Margaret Kohl. Minneapolis: Fortress, 1993.

Olitzky, Kerry M., and Daniel Judson. *Jewish Ritual: A Brief Introduction for Christians*. Woodstock, VT: Jewish Lights, 2006.

Osborn, Eric. *Ethical Patterns in Early Christian Thought*. Cambridge: Cambridge University Press, 1976.

Parmiter, John. *Ten at Work: Living the Commandments in Your Job*. Nottingham, UK: InterVarsity, 2011.

Pew Research Center. "America's Changing Religious Landscape." http://www.pewforum.org/2015/05/12/americas-changing-religious-landscape/.

Pfeffer, Jeffrey. *Power: Why Some People Have It – and Others Don't*. New York: HarperCollins, 2010.

Pierce, Gregory F. Augustine. *Finding God@Work: Practicing Spirituality in Your Workplace*. Plainfield, NJ: RENEW International, 2006.

"Population Clock." https://www.census.gov.

Reed, Esther D. *Work, for God's Sake: Christian Ethics in the Workplace*. London: Darton, Longman and Todd, 2010.

Rohr, Richard, with Mike Morrell. *The Divine Dance: The Trinity and Your Transformation*. New Kensington, PA: Whitaker House, 2016.

Sasse, Ben. *The Vanishing American Adult: Our Coming-of-Age Crisis – and How to Rebuild a Culture of Self-Reliance*. New York: St. Martin's, 2017.

Satlow, Michael L. *Creating Judaism: History, Tradition, Practice*. New York: Columbia University Press, 2006.

Sayers, Dorothy L. *Creed or Chaos? Why Christians Must Choose Either Dogma or Disaster (Or, Why it Really Does Matter What You Believe)*. Manchester, NH: Sophia Institute, 1999.

Scurlock, Robin, and Steve Goss. *I Love My Work: Six Studies to Help Churches Understand and Equip Christians in the Workplace*. Bradford-on-Avon, UK: Terra Nova, 2002.

Shattock, Geoff. *Wake Up to Work: Friendship and Faith in the Workplace.* Bletchley, UK: Scripture Union, 2000.

Sherman, Doug, and William Hendricks. *Your Work Matters to God.* Colorado Springs, CO: NavPress, 1987.

Stevens, R. Paul. *The Other Six Days: Vocation, Work, and Ministry in Biblical Perspective.* Grand Rapids: Eerdmans, 2000.

————. *Work Matters: Lessons from Scripture.* Grand Rapids: Eerdmans, 2012.

Telushkin, Joseph. *Jewish Literacy.* New York: William Morrow, 2008.

Troeltsch, Ernst. *The Social Teaching of the Christian Churches.* Translated by Olive Wyon. New York: Macmillan, 1931.

Vaidyanathan, Brandon, and Patricia Snell. "Motivations for and Obstacles to Religious Financial Giving," *Sociology of Religion,* 72.2 (2011) 189–214. https://doi: 10.1093/socrel/srq074.

Volf, Miroslav. *Work in the Spirit: Toward a Theology of Work.* Eugene, OR: Wipf and Stock, 2001.

Walker, Joe W. *Money in the Church.* Edited by Alan K. Waltz. Nashville: Abingdon, 1982.

Wallace, Ronald S. *Calvin's Doctrine of the Christian Life.* Grand Rapids: Eerdmans, 1959.

Wesley, John. *John Wesley's Sermons: An Anthology.* Edited by Albert C. Outler and Richard P. Heitzenrater. Nashville: Abingdon, 1991.

West, Philip. "Karl Barth's Theology of Work: A Resource for the Late 1980s." *Modern Churchman* 30.3 (1988) 13–19.

Wingren, Gustaf. *Luther on Vocation.* Translated by Carl C. Rasmussen. Eugene, OR: Wipf and Stock, 2004.

Wynne, Jago. *Working Without Wilting: Starting Well to Finish Strong.* Nottingham, UK: InterVarsity, 2009.

Subject Index

Scripture Index

CPSIA information can be obtained
at www.ICGtesting.com
Printed in the USA
JSHW020835180919
1513JS00002B/3